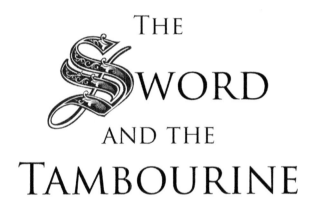

THE SWORD
AND THE
TAMBOURINE

HANNA E. FARWELL

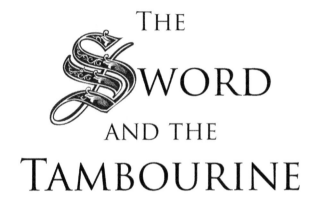

THE SWORD AND THE TAMBOURINE

BECOMING A WARRIOR THROUGH WORSHIP

DESTINY IMAGE, PUBLISHERS, INC.
P.O. Box 310, Shippensburg, PA 17257-0310
"Speaking to the Purposes of God for This Generation and for the Generations to Come."

This book and all other Destiny Image, Revival Press, MercyPlace, Fresh Bread, Destiny Image Fiction, and Treasure House books are available at Christian bookstores and distributors worldwide.

For a U.S. bookstore nearest you, call 1-800-722-6774.
For more information on foreign distributors, call 717-532-3040.
Reach us on the Internet: www.destinyimage.com.

Trade Paper ISBN 13: 978-0-7684-3595-5
Hardcover ISBN 13: 978-0-7684-3596-2
Large Print ISBN 13: 978-0-7684-3597-9
Ebook ISBN 13: 978-0-7684-9053-4

For Worldwide Distribution, Printed in the U.S.A.
1 2 3 4 5 6 7 8 9 10 11 / 13 12 11 10

DEDICATION

This book is dedicated to all those who bravely enlist in the Lord's army and want to do great exploits for Him.

> *...You are to help your brothers until the Lord gives them rest, as He has done for you, and until they too have taken possession of the land that the Lord your God is giving them...* (Joshua 1:14-15).

ACKNOWLEDGMENTS

My first thanks go to You, Lord. Thank You for allowing me into the secret chambers and letting me write what I hear from You. Thank You for the all-surpassing privilege of being welcomed into Your presence to worship before Your throne. I can truly say that *"better is one day in Your courts than a thousand elsewhere..."* (Ps. 84:10).

My second thank-you goes to my husband, Jeff, and our children. It has taken me hundreds of hours to put this manuscript together, hours that I planned in as discreetly as I could between chores, homeschooling, and caring for family needs. I am grateful for the grace they have given me to write. Thank you, Jeff, for editing a very lengthy manuscript, paying attention to the details, and helping cut it down to size. You made it much better! Thank you also for blessing a fatigued wife in the evenings. You keep proving that you are a man after God's own heart!

Thank you, my wonderful children—Josef, Joy, John, Hosea, Hosanna, Host, Christina, Calvary, Caleb, and Gabriel—for making this venture a joy by your willingness to accept a busy mom.

Third, I want to say thank you to the great people who have come alongside me to read, edit, and comment on this lengthy manuscript. Erin Girouex, thank you for helping me with grammar and editing. You have been such a blessing to me! Glenn Pearson, a pastor of 30 years and an author himself (*Prepare to Meet Your God*), took the time to read the complete manuscript and scan for theological inaccuracies and errors. Thank you, Glenn, for this invaluable help! I am so thankful to have been able to change some sections of the book before it went to print!

Len and Diane Stitt were leaders of our team during the two years my family served overseas and experienced many of the things written about in this book. Len shared a number of stories with me to further illustrate the power of team worship. For this, and for the deep impact they have had on my life, I will always be grateful. Thank you, Len and Diane. I love you.

Jenny Mayhew has been my main source and personal contact with the beautiful movement called *Ministry to Jesus*. She is a quiet woman who has been entrusted with great things by our God. Thank you, Jenny, for your labor of love and for your help with this book project.

Dale and Jill Borgelt are not only personal friends, but they also poured themselves out for our sake when our family went overseas, to pray for us, help us with newsletters, and support us in any way they could to see us succeed on the field. Jill has been medicine to my heart every time I have come in contact with her, bringing encouragement and life by her attitude and words. After our return to the states, Dale reviewed a number of chapters of this book while he himself battled bone cancer. These friends have extended one of the most precious friendships we have ever experienced. They also live a lifestyle of worship and warfare that is the epitome of what I am writing about. Thank you, Dale and Jill, for your dedication to the Lord and for blessing us so greatly.

Jon and Mickie Harvie are long-standing friends who have hosted our family numerous times—and months on end—to see us off and on the field. Considering their and our large families, that is no small feat! Under their roof I sat many hours working on this book. Thank you, dear friends, for your lavish grace and sacrifice to help us out.

Jeff and I were blessed by the Lord with the forging of new friendships upon our return to Nebraska soil. David and Joanne Norton and Gary Neve have come and worshiped in our home and have become our "team" on the home front. They are a particular blessing to us in that Joanne and Gary are veteran spiritual "mappers" (and Dave an incredible servant!), helping us track down and understand our new assignments from the Lord. They brought some valuable input into Chapter 9 of this book, where I share on the value of spiritual research and breaking regional darkness. Thank you for your help, fellow warriors!

Finally, I want to thank the people at Destiny Image for helping us launch into a new kind of ministry through the written word and for their expert help and valuable input. Special thanks, Marti Statler and Dean Drawbaugh, our personal contacts at DI, for your support and encouragement and for seeing potential in this book project. We feel we have not found just a publishing house, but also long-lasting friends.

DISCLAIMER

In one message, Derek Prince said, "I cannot communicate what I do not understand. But I will not let the things I *don't* understand keep me from the things I *do* understand."[1] This book is a compilation of the things I have started to understand. I am not a trained scholar, neither am I tremendously "spiritual." When I started this book at the Lord's bidding, I spent the mornings with my team in worship. The rest of the day was spent supervising school for my children and trying to keep above the surface of household chores and caring for my young children. At the time of completing this book project, I am again busy with home schooling and cooking for my large family, with only occasional chances to be involved in corporate worship times.

There would be scores of you who would know more and have greater experiences on several of the topics presented in these pages. But the Lord asked me to put my observations, the revelation He has granted, and my own experiences into writing. This is the result. It is not exhaustive and could easily be added to. My hope in writing this book is to encourage others to seek for and embrace their destiny as children and warriors of God and to train them for the times of intense battle that lie ahead. I personally see worship as the primary way to not only stay healthy, but also flourishing and active in this new time period we have entered, and so I have shared those insights that have been the most helpful in my own life. May it speed your learning and your growth.

I quote authors and speakers Derek Prince and Rick Joyner numerous times in the pages of this book. I am not intending to favor their teachings or set them above other excellent resources. It just so happened that while developing my own understanding on spiritual warfare and the importance of the current times, these two were available with their materials to influence me and to confirm my experiences and what I personally had heard from the Lord. I am grateful for their wisdom and their ministries.

ENDNOTE

1. Derek Prince, audio message titled "Curses—the Cause."

Endorsements

These are uncertain times. In the season that we are living in, we need clear, understandable instruction about what we are facing and how to prepare for it. Hanna Farwell provides that basic instruction using her knowledge of Scripture and her personal experience. Read and be prepared for your destiny.

Lonnie Parton
Pastor, Victory Fellowship, Iowa
Author, *Desperate People in Desperate Times*

Is Hanna's book for you? If you have a desire to *"press on toward the goal for the prize of the upward call of God in Christ Jesus"* (Phil. 3:14 NKJV)—a call to spiritual maturity incumbent upon all believers—this volume will be a most valuable resource. Hanna does much more than document sound biblical theology on the vitally important topic of spiritual maturity. She also exhibits multiple profiles of true Christian maturity based on practical "walking-it-out" dynamics drawn from the deep well of her personal experience of serving Jesus as a wife, mother, "missionary" to her own family at home, and missionary to the family of God stateside and abroad. So if you truly desire to go from faith to faith; from strength to strength; from fruit to more fruit and on to much fruit (see John 15); from glory to glory; from dissipating zeal to being aglow and ablaze with the Holy Spirit; from a somewhat dull "plateau Christianity" to living on Mount Zion as an "overcomer" capable of being "more than a conqueror"; you need this book! Take it home. Read it. Study it. Pray it, and become better equipped to be an effective laborer in the end-time harvest reaching precious souls for the glory of Jesus!

Glenn Pearson
Pastor, Missionary, Teacher
Author, *Prepare to Meet Your God, Scriptural Meditations for the Terminally Ill & Their Caregivers*

The Sword and the Tambourine offers a unique look at worship and intercession and the vital role they play *together* in the believer's life. After reading this book, I walked away provoked by the Holy Spirit that we, as lovers of Christ, are not only called to fight through worship and prayer, but to overcome! If you're just starting out in the faith or you're a veteran believer, you will be challenged and stirred by this book.

Emily Baker
Worship leader at Victory Fellowship Church
Council Bluffs, Iowa

Hanna Farwell's book will open your eyes to the battle we are living in and encourage you to "live a life of worship" *as* warfare. She insightfully lays out before us the chump tactics of our enemy and points us to our victorious King and His rock-solid truths and life-saving strategies—we need to align ourselves with Him and be more than conquerors!

Jennifer Hunter
Worshiper with *Harp and Bowl ministry*

I have been working as a spiritual mapper for nearly a dozen years, regionally, nationally, and internationally. Hanna's description of spiritual mapping—its purpose, challenges, goals, and resulting transformation in neighborhoods, communities, and nations—is very accurate. It gives a very clear picture of how we all as researchers, intercessors, prayer walkers, worshipers, and prophets may work together as part of our Heavenly Father's army.

Joanne Norton
Spiritual mapper
Omaha, Nebraska

The Sword and the Tambourine challenges the reader to go beyond the basics of the Christian walk by giving insights and many practical examples of living, not just talking, your faith.

Gary Neve
Warrior in the army of Jesus, Omaha, Nebraska

Having watched and learned from Hanna's humble position in the Lord, submission to the living God, and earthly submission to her husband, I have seen her worship and finding the presence of the Lord. As He gives revelation, He takes her into battle areas unknown for the breaking down of strongholds over her home, her family, and her city. It is from this experience that she is most able to pass along to us wisdom, courage, and discernment so that we might come to learn our own place in worship and in war.

Diane Bilek
Spiritual mapper/Worship warrior

The Sword and the Tambourine was honed by real experiences in the frontlines of South Asia. Jeff and Hanna Farwell have been practitioners of the spiritual principles they write about. This book will be an important contribution to strengthening the intercessory prayer lives of God's spiritual warriors.

Len and Diane Stitt
Missionaries

CONTENTS

INTRODUCTION

The voice of the Lord will shatter Assyria; with His scepter He will strike them down. Every stroke the Lord lays on them with His punishing rod will be to the music of tambourines and harps, as He fights them in battle with the blows of His arm (Isaiah 30:31-32).

There are scores of excellent books on the market covering spiritual warfare. There are many more that instruct and challenge the believer to prayer and worship. This book is not written with the intent of laying that foundation again. It is written for the purpose of preparing God's people for the battles and the harvests of the approaching end of this age.

Many times there has been a gap in our thinking between *war* and *worship*. But the two really need to go hand in hand to become what the Lord intended it to be—the force and power of the Holy Spirit moving through human vessels to prepare the way for His coming. A doctor who spends all his time with sick people becomes weary and forgets that there is health and beauty in life. In the same way, a soldier who keeps fighting becomes drained and gets the feeling that the battle is endless and the enemy too strong. It is worship that brings back his perspective. Worship without warfare, by contrast, can become diluted to self-centered sessions of having our needs met and a polishing of our swords just to put them back in their sheaths unused. On the one hand, true worship prepares us for battle and renews our strength that we may persevere, and this happens while all our attention and devotion is fixed on our Lord, the Commander. Inspired warfare, on the other hand, destroys the work of satan, accomplishes the purposes of God on earth, and displays Jesus to mankind so that He may be known, loved, and feared.

Once a man or woman or child takes up the sword, worship takes on its rightful shape. Never again will this person be content to sing a song and call it worship. When a man realizes that his sword is real and that he has been taken into His service, he will never again want to speak flippantly to the Lord, to satan and his demons, or to people. He who gave the task is watching. So are the heavenly hosts. So are the saints who have entered Heaven. So are the evil spirits who now have to rethink their strategies. Before a man understands his weapons, he imagines what it would be like to carry authority; he pretends he knows the deep things of God; he hides his ignorance with clever theories and words. But once he gets that sword and feels the weight of it in his hand and realizes he has found favor with God—he plays no more, he pretends no more, he hides no more. He receives his orders, he puts on his armor, and he goes to war. When he worships, he worships as a soldier. He glorifies his Commander, rejoices in the ultimate victory, and keeps his ears open for a word, for direction, for the next mission. *Whatever it is, Lord, I am ready, willing, and able by Your power. Speak it, Lord. I am listening. What is on Your radar screen? What's the next move? What do You want me to do?*

Recently, my husband Jeff and I, together with our children, had the great privilege for two years to be a part of an overseas organization that gives the first hours of every workday to worship and seeking the Lord. Even before our joining we had started to appreciate the great importance of worship to see spiritual victory and breakthrough happen. But since joining our team, we saw even clearer how crucial our times of worship were for receiving guidance and for remaining healthy in a dark, oppressive land. We found that our task before the Lord was to break open the "skies of brass" and establish His Kingdom through adoration and giving Him the firstfruits of our time. We were not asking for one or two souls to be rescued from the suffocating lies of the enemy; we wanted the glory and light of Jesus to change the nation!

There are different seasons in human history. The earth saw a glorious creation and then the awful fall of mankind into sin. It saw the time of Noah, when righteousness was nearly extinct, it saw the call of the Israelite nation and later her continuous rebellion toward God during the time of the kings and the prophets. It saw the silence between the Testaments and the time of Christ. This time, the time of Christ, when the light and purposes of God were manifest in the flesh, also saw a great amount of open demonic manifestation to combat His advancement. Then came the time of the apostles and the rapid spread of Christianity, which satan combated furiously. With the spread of the Gospel, the enemy presented seductions, and within a few hundred years, the powerful fire that God had lit on the earth was being smothered. The alternative "gospel" of Islam was introduced and reconquered vast territories for the realm of darkness. In other places, the truths of God were institutionalized and became void of power. Thus, the world saw a time of great blackness, which we now call the *Dark Ages*. It was followed by the Reformation and the breath of God to awaken the Church. Following this was the missionary movement, which again saw great advancements for the Kingdom of God. Since then the world has seen the age of technology and the idolizing of knowledge above the friendship of God.

Then what shall we call this era, this age? In the Church for these last 15 years or so, something new and strange has sprung up that we have not seen before. I believe this is the age of the call of God to take up arms and go to war against the hosts of darkness. This is the generation of Joshuas and Calebs who insist on confronting the giants and seeing their fellow brothers receive their inheritance. This is the age of spiritual authority that breaks open the dark places of the earth and frees captives; it is the age that sees the hand of God move in unprecedented miracles and partakes of the glorious harvest of the endtimes. This era will see the power that eventually draws out the antichrist to take his last stand. It is the time of the preparation for the coming of Christ.

Any age can last for hundreds of years, depending on God's divine intervention and man's response to Him. I am not saying that His return is imminent, but *soon*. He is who He is. He will come when He comes. But we must be wise and read the times (see Matt. 16:2-3; 24:32) and move as His Spirit directs.

What I lay out before you in this book is what I believe to be the key to fulfilling our destiny as the Joshua generation. It will be accomplished with a sword in one hand and a tambourine in the other—by the power of the quickening word of God on our lips and His high praises on our tongues. Do you want to be a part of this? Do you dare take God at His Word and press into unchartered, even enemy, territory? Do you want a heart like David's, he who slew the lion and the bear? Do you want to face giants in the name of the Lord and see them fall? Do you want to recapture what the enemy has stolen from those you love? Do you want to have a part in the transformation of nations? Do you want to participate in the glory and exultation from a battle being won for your God? Do you want to learn how to wield the sword of the Spirit, which is sharp enough to cut through the bondages of hell? Do you want to embrace your destiny as the son or as the daughter of the Most High God?

Then come. He will train your hands for war.

Praise the Lord.

Sing to the Lord a new song, His praise in the assembly of the saints.

Let Israel rejoice in their Maker; let the people of Zion be glad in their King.

Let them praise His name with dancing and make music to Him with tambourine and harp.

For the Lord takes delight in His people; He crowns the humble with salvation.

Let the saints rejoice in this honor and sing for joy on their beds.

May the praise of God be in their mouths and a double-edged sword in their hands,

to inflict vengeance on the nations and punishment on the peoples, to bind their kings with fetters, their nobles with shackles of iron, to carry out the sentence written against them.

This is the glory of all His saints.

Praise the Lord

(Psalm 149).

CHAPTER ONE

WE MUST FIGHT!

ave you ever wondered why you are here, at this point in time? Have you questioned the need to stay on the earth after you were saved? I mean, couldn't we all just accept Jesus and head straight for Heaven instead of staying down here in mortal bodies, in sweat and daily routines and work, sometimes fighting to stay above the clamor and piles of things waiting for our attention? Have you sometimes felt like you were walking in a fog, as if the skies themselves were pressing you to live *ordinary*, while the spirit in you cried for eyes to see and a heart to understand what really goes on from God's perspective?

You were born for destiny. We live on the very seam between one age and the next. Already in the last few years there have been dramatic increases in earthquakes, flooding, and other natural disasters, acting as a warning sign to the Church that it is time to arise. Many godly people are speaking up and declaring that the Lord has started the preparation for the last days. There will be increasing darkness in the world, but also increasing glory for His people.

The Lord said 2,000 years ago, *"Many are invited, but few are chosen"* (Matt. 22:14; see also Rev. 17:14). We are invited to go deep in fellowship with the Lord, and if we do, He will also choose us to partake of a glorious destiny. The time for sleep is over; it is time to arise. May He now open our eyes to see what has been hidden from us before; may we come to see the glory of Heaven and the plans of the enemy. May we find our weapons and know our provisions. May we find friends and prepare for our missions. And most of all, may we come to know the Lord in a new way. For in these days He will become known as *the Commander of the armies of the Lord*, the Lord of Hosts.

WELCOME TO REALITY

Those who have not seen war situations too often and not at their front doors are often lulled to believe that we live in a rather nice and kind world. A Western mentality toward evil is that it somehow is not supposed to up-set our private lives, and if it does, it is seen as an uncommon tragedy. The subject of a real satan and demonic activities seems very out of place and definitely extreme in our cozy living rooms. It is so easy to accept the mate-rial world and so difficult to believe in the reality of the spiritual realm.

Other parts of the world have adopted different mind frames. The Afri-can people, with their long history of animistic practices, know too well that there are evil forces at large. The Arabic world is full of demonic appearances and curses while their god stays aloft and impersonal. Even in the West, which now accepts atheism and materialism as reality, many are seeking alternative sources of power since the Church seems void of it—witches, warlocks, and cults are becoming increasingly popular. Life without a pow-erful God who orders the universe and has a purpose for our lives is not life at all. It becomes an empty pursuit for personal gain and the opening of our senses to anything that attracts.

As believers in Jesus Christ, the risen Son of God, we have the privi-lege of learning the mysteries and the reality of the unseen realms and of beginning to understand what in the world is going on here on the blue planet and the skies above it. There is no way we would be able to find this out on our own, even if we spent the rest of our lives looking for it. But because we're the adopted sons and daughters of God, He starts revealing it to us. It changes our worldview for good.

The first important step we take on the walk of faith is accepting that Jesus is who He claims to be and accepting His offer for forgiveness of sins. Then our newly acquired faith is put to the test with the Scriptures, the Bible, to accept it as God's eternal and irrevocable Word. "Sure, I believe it," we say innocently—and then we are bombarded on all sides with all kinds of information, questions, and doubts. We think, we pray, we research, and we question. Finally we are back at the beginning again—faith. Either Jesus is God, or He is not. If He is not, then he is a liar and a deceiver, or maybe a lunatic with a big head, thinking he is God. If not, then He must be who He says He is.[1] And if He *is* God, then we have to accept His words; first of all because He is God and He knows everything, and secondly, because if we can not trust God (especially the kind of God who just saved you at the cost of His own life) then who can we trust? Without this immovable rock of certainty, life has no real foundation and values become subject to personal taste.

Once we take this step of trust, we find that our faith is validated many times over. God starts showing up in the strangest or the most normal circumstances. His answers sometimes come so precisely in the right time and in such amazing ways that our faith doubles in a heartbeat. The joy of our salvation and newfound assurance is throbbing in our chest, a pulsating new life within that cannot be matched with any other exhilarating experience— could it be that the Holy Spirit has moved in to live in us?

And it is at this point that suddenly the world, our "home ground," starts to change in front of our eyes. Not that anything is changing except us—we are just now starting to notice things on a different plane. It is the Spirit who is sensitizing us to notice the invisible. At the same time, another miracle is occurring. The boring, hard-to-understand Bible text starts jumping out at us—a new revelation, a sudden understanding of something that before seemed irrelevant or strange. Something small we thought of one day finds its explanation in His Word the next. How strange! How come we did not notice before?

The Bible is a big, heavy book that anybody could buy and read. It is not encrypted, *yet it is!* God, who made our intellects, has done what no computer hacker is able to do: make it so hard to understand that the most brilliant scholar cannot understand its meaning, but at the same time so simple that a child can learn the truth (see 1 Cor. 1:18-25). It is a locked-up secret to those who approach it in the wrong way, but at the same instant, it is wide open to the open-hearted—the amazing, deep secrets of God hidden in the pages of the Bible, ours for the taking.

Why am I saying all this? Simply because without this foundation, the rest of what I will share will not make sense at all. There is another reality around us, the invisible one, and we get to know it by the Word of God and by revelation from the Holy Spirit.

You may wonder, is it necessary to get to know this part of reality? If it is unseen, is it not best left alone; shouldn't we just wait for Heaven? Then God can explain things in detail, and we can not get misled. I agree; that would be more pleasant, if it were not for a few little details...

First of all, there was more to your acceptance of Christ as Savior than what you maybe initially understood. You suddenly changed your allegiance to a different Master, and you have changed sides in an all-out war between two kingdoms. Second, your former master—whether you knew he existed or not—does not like that you have switched sides. In fact, he hates what you have done and has decided to take you out. Third, you may have switched sides and been rescued from the eternal fires, but you are still in enemy territory and will continue to be so for the rest of your earthly life (see Col. 1:13; John 15:18-20; 1 Pet. 5:8; Ps. 2:1-3; James 4:4; 2 Pet. 2:9).

I am sorry if this shocks you, but the Bible states it in war terms, and it is the best explanation we will get for what is actually happening in the invisible realm (see 2 Cor. 10:3-4; 1 Pet. 2:11; Ps. 144:1; 2 Tim. 2:3; Eph. 6:10-13). With all these facts at hand, would you like to know what is happening, or do you want to walk blindfolded through life and just hope to not attract attention? To speak candidly, our best chance for survival and success will be to learn quickly what is happening around us and get caught up to speed on the scenario we were just made aware of. Like, *who is my enemy? How many troops does he have, and where are the ones that are the closest to me? How can I recognize what he is up to? What has the Lord given me to protect myself with? Do I have any weapons? Any mode of communication? Do I have any food rations handy? Do I have any guys around who are on my team? What is it that I am supposed to be doing? Do I get anything as a reward if I enlist to work for Him here behind enemy lines? Do I have any assurance that I can get out of this alive?*

Good. I am glad you are asking. As unreal as it may seem, you are on the verge of stepping into a reality that will far supersede your wildest wishes for adventure and yet keep your heart in the deep, abiding peace of Jesus our Commander.

Oh, and one more thing—welcome to reality.

Unlocking the Scriptures

The Word of God is likened to food (see Matt. 4:4). Through diligent study and revelation from the Holy Spirit, we are nourished in our inner person, and we are thrust out of spiritual infancy into the beginnings of maturity (see 1 Cor. 3:1-2; Heb. 5:13-14). The goal of our growth is Christ-likeness.

The whole Bible is food, the Old Testament as well as the New Testament. It does not matter what age we live in or how many thousands of years ago it was written—God wrote it for *us,* to be our food and sustenance. He chose to have it written *that* way, and through it He will train us for life here as well as prepare us for the life to come. He could have put in a whole lot more (see John 21:25), but this is what He chose to give. This is now our personal handbook and daily provision.

The Bible is a locked book for our understanding until we approach it with the right attitude and the Holy Spirit sheds light on it. But when we come to truly hear from God, we will find layer after layer of meaning and depth opening up to us! The Scriptures are amazing because they were inspired by the God who creates every snowflake unique, counts every hair on our heads, and calls every star by name (see Matt. 10:30; Ps. 147:4). It should not surprise us, then, that His Word seems to increase in depth and beauty as our minds are enlightened.

The Lord wrote Scriptures for people; therefore, He wrote it in a way that we can understand—He is speaking our language, so to speak. This is usually referred to as *literal interpretation.* If we read one of the historic books, we read it as history—we take in the story and meditate on the plot and the people. We learn how God thinks and responds, what He loves, and what He hates. We learn about humanity's response to God and to other people. It is simply reading the text at face value and trying to figure out where, when, how, and why. It is a study of characters and drawing out the lessons and applications that were placed in the text for our edification (see 2 Tim. 3:16).

But—God did more than speak our language! He wants to come and meet us where we are, but after fellowship has been restored, He wants to bring us up to experience things from His perspective. To help us know Him, we must start learning *His* language!

God's heavenly language is largely visual or pictorial. That means He uses pictures and symbols to show us how He views things. This we will refer to as *symbolic interpretation,* and we can see evidence of its use in how Jesus primarily spoke in parables and in how the prophets would see visions that were full of symbolic language (see Matt. 13:35; Luke 8:10). The heavenly language is meant to confound the wisdom of the world and still be unlocked to those who draw near to God (see 1 Cor. 1:19-25; Matt. 11:25-27). Once we taste of this heavenly language, it becomes a treasure to our hearts.

It is good to start at "The Parable of the Sower" in Mark 4, which the Lord used as a doorway to help us start interpreting the heavenly language.

After Jesus told this parable, the disciples asked for its interpretation. He answered, *"Don't you understand this parable? How then will you understand any parable?"* (Mark 4:13). He then gave them the meaning of the parable, thus showing them how to interpret.

A parable or a symbolic message is uncovered by replacing an object with its meaning. With this I do not mean a literal translation of the word or a word study, but finding the main characteristic of the object, the one thing above other things it is known for or associated with. Most physical objects have a primary symbolic meaning (a *root* meaning), and from this root there could be several possible *branch* meanings. For example, the root meaning in dream language for *sheep* is "innocent." But *sheep* could also point to *defenseless, gentle, God's people,* or *unsaved people;* these would then be the branch meanings.

The first task is to find the root meaning of the symbol. Many objects, whether animate or inanimate, will have keys laid out somewhere in Scripture.

Most symbols have a meaning that is derived from the basic characteristic of the object. Say that we want to find out the symbolic meaning of *lion.* First we look for its mention in Scripture. We find that it at times represents Jesus (the Lion of Judah, see Rev. 5:5) and sometimes satan (a lion that roars and devours, see 1 Pet. 5:8). We remember that a lion is most often referred to as "the king of the animal world" and is seen as majestic. We could, therefore, set a tentative root meaning of *lion* to be "king," or "ruler," whether good or bad.

The use of the heavenly language is valid in many more areas than just Scripture reading. God uses His visual language in so many places. One prevalent place where He speaks symbolically is in dreams.

Say that I dream about talking on my cell phone. I am not going to find *cell phone* mentioned in the Bible, but I know that its primary function is *communication.* Depending on how the dream went, I can now decipher the Lord's message. For example, talking on the phone with a sister with constant static breaking up the words could mean that the situation is so charged that good communication is hindered.

Symbols are also everywhere around us in creation. It is all in picture form—pictures that help us understand how the Lord sees things.

Unlocking the Scriptures is for the purpose of learning to understand how God speaks, whether He is speaking our language or is using His own. The more we study the Scriptures and the heavenly language, the more we will delight in the wealth of His wisdom and amazing ways. We are getting to know Him more!

INTERPRETING SYMBOLS: AN EXAMPLE

We are now going to look at a Bible text to learn more of how to interpret symbols.

> When the Lord your God brings you into the land you are entering to possess and drives out before you many nations—the Hittites, Girgashites, Amorites, Canaanites, Perizzites, Hivites and Jebusites, seven nations larger and stronger than you—and when the Lord your God has delivered them over to you and you have defeated them, then you must destroy them totally. Make no treaty with them, and show them no mercy (Deuteronomy 7:1-2).

We first look at the names mentioned to see if we can find out their meaning. Sometimes this is easy, and sometimes it is hard to find. A pastor I know researched this passage and compiled the following meanings:

1. Hittites—Fear

2. Girgashites—Strangers from God

3. Amorites—Murdering words

4. Canaanites—Depression

5. Perizzites—Lack of commitment

6. Hivites—Compromise

7. Jebusites—Heaviness[2]

Next we look for a symbolic meaning in the circumstances given. This text does not prove too hard because the New Testament speaks of its spiritual application.

As believers in Jesus, we have been grafted into the true Israel, the people of God. We are part of the people to whom God is speaking (see Rom. 9:6-8). Israel came out of Egypt, the "house of slavery"—Egypt symbolizes our sinful state before salvation (see Heb. 11:24-27; Matt. 2:15). Christ redeemed us by His blood in the same way that the first Passover happened in Egypt (see Exod. 12:21-30; 1 Cor. 5:7). Now we are in the desert. God has not popped us right into the Promised Land because He wanted to train us and have us ready to claim our inheritance. He does want us to make it into *our* Promised Land though—which is not Heaven after we die, but our inheritance, our place in His Kingdom, and our promised allotment from God. God does not enjoy seeing us spend our time here on earth just safely out of sin and surviving; He wants us to march into our destiny, where we will be joyful and strong in Him.

Interpreting symbols in this text unlocked a message from the Lord to us as believers. These are the enemies He wants us to be ruthless with—*fear, alienation from God, hatred toward people, depression, lack of commitment, compromise, and heaviness.* They are not flesh and blood, but they will try to hinder us from receiving our inheritance! God says we must destroy their hold on our lives, or they will hinder us from living according to God's plans.

With some persistence in asking the Lord for revelation and applying ourselves in the interpretation of symbols, we will find that the Word of

God is wonderfully applicable to our modern day and to the problems and circumstances we face.

It might seem that symbolic language is confusing, easy to misunderstand, and easy to misinterpret. If there are several possible meanings, would we not be prone to choose whatever interpretation seems the most convenient to us?

Do not worry. This is God's language, and He knows what He is saying. Therefore, the interpretation is only valid if it shows His thoughts or intent. We can learn the heavenly language and all the symbols, but interpretation belongs to God (see Gen. 40:8). It is by the revelation of the Holy Spirit that the true meaning becomes clear to us. This is done on purpose so that we will only know the Lord and His will to the extent that we seek Him and not special knowledge. Just as a puzzle does not look right until the pieces are in place, so we can often tell when we are missing the true message. It just doesn't have the confirming nudge of the Holy Spirit.

Although it is true that symbolic language easily throws us for a curve and can be mystifying, the Lord is very pleased with us for searching out these matters (see Prov. 25:2).

We will find good help on the road by reading God's Word for both its literal and its symbolic message. We will discover more and more how timeless and useful the truths are—it is still the same enemy, and the same war is still raging. The Old Testament can become a great encouragement in our unseen war as we start recognizing how the battle scenes give us patterns for how we are to fight our spiritual battles.

As you study, take hold of the truths He gives. Have your notebook handy, write in the margin beside the verse that sticks out to you, and start a habit of underlining the verses that make an impression. Bear in mind that God's Word is food. Reading quickly is like smelling the food rather than partaking. It will sink into your heart as you study, ponder, write down, memorize, meditate, and pray.

Do not lean on reason to guide you through your reading, but open your heart to receive, as you would food. I was at a seminar once in which the speaker quoted Corrie ten Boom as saying, "The Bible is like a bar of chocolate—it is meant to be eaten and enjoyed, not analyzed." Eat, loved one. He wants your inner person strong. *I Am the Lord your God, who brought you up out of Egypt. Open wide your mouth and I will fill it* (Ps. 81:10).

No Neutral Ground

In the Second World War, Hitler's troops kept marching through countries, conquering and obliterating any resistance while exterminating the Jewish people. In history class in Sweden, we read about the fleeing Jews and how it was tremendously dangerous to help them escape their destruction. On the one hand the Norwegian people showed great bravery in hiding and aiding these Jews as well as defending their country. Sweden, on the other hand, declared itself neutral to avoid bloodshed and let the Nazi troops march through the country on their missions. We escaped personal pain, but at the cost of someone else's.

There is no neutral ground in the war for our souls. Jesus said, *"He who is not with Me is against Me, and he who does not gather with Me, scatters"* (Luke 11:23). To not engage in your stand for the Lord is to serve the purposes of our enemy. To do evil is sin, but it is also a sin to see the good that needs to be done and not do it (see Prov. 3:27; James 2:14-18; 1 John 3:17-18).

We cannot serve two masters. We cannot serve *no* master, either. We may think we are doing what *we* want to do, but satan twists culture to serve his will. If we serve ourselves, we serve the sinful nature, which serves his desire. There is no fence to straddle between the Kingdom of Light and the kingdom of darkness.

Satan's plans are to kill, destroy, or neutralize all who oppose his rule. If we are content to remain spiritual infants, only caring for our own needs, then he will gladly torment us from time to time, but we are no real threat to him. But when we start growing spiritually and bearing fruit, we will start noticing some resistance. It may come as tiredness, pride, distraction, sickness, or discouragement. Satan sends it, and the Lord allows it; one means to stop us, the other to push us to a greater level of awareness and endurance to fight. This is basic boot camp. We must press through and not let anything distract us from moving forward.

We have many growing children in our home. The older ones are becoming preteens, and my husband Jeff and I have started handing them more responsibilities. But since they are not used to the workload or their new chores, they often complain. "This is too difficult! I can't do it. Why can't he (or she) do it?" Many times we act the same way toward what God hands us through circumstances. It is hard to keep giving when we are tired. It is hard to trust when the doctors show the statistics. It is hard to step out in faith when life stops being theoretical and new circumstances push our convictions in our faces and demand action. But there is no other way to grow faith and spiritual strength; muscles need to be exercised to become strong and useful. God loves His children and delights in His little ones; but, as someone once pointed out, it is not so cute if a 20-year-old still needs to be spoon fed. For our own sake, for the sake of those we love, and for the sake of the lost, we need to grow up and shoulder the cross the Lord gives us. And since we do not know how much will be required of us, let us train to excel in the worst-case scenarios!

CALLED TO FIGHT

Throughout the New Testament, the Lord commands His followers to take action. In a time when we are lulled to sleep by our vast resources of entertainment and information, we must quiet ourselves to be able to heed the call of the Holy Spirit. When we do, He can push us into Kingdom action.

The laws of the universe may serve us as an example here. The second law of thermodynamics speaks of order and disorder in the universe: *All systems unattended go toward chaos (disorder).* It is, therefore, necessary to bring order to a system to keep its quality. The only reason I remember this law is because of my father, a passionate physics teacher.

"Everybody to the living room!" he would yell while ringing the bell in our home, and the thunder of 12 or so pairs of feet—depending on the year—followed seconds later.

"Guess what I found—a *not so clean* sock on the living room floor! And whose are these books? And this toy here? And these *school papers?* Let me tell you *the second law of thermo dynamics!*" He would tell us the law, and then add, "This house will not clean itself! Look!" He would drop a toy to the floor. "Amazing—all things tend to go to the lowest place, and it is going to take *someone* to get it back to its assigned place. And that *someone* is going to be *you!*"

Yes, it is us. If we want to advance spiritually, we must be willing to discipline ourselves and accept training. The Christian life is not stagnant. The Lord says that we are to "gather" with Him. If we do not want to put our attention on doing what He calls us to do, but instead focus on the affairs of life, Jesus does not just see us as absent from work, but actually counteracting what He is doing (see Luke 11:23). I am not talking about running around trying to do things all the time just to be sure we are doing something. I am talking about being responsible in doing what the Lord has personally told us to care for. If we are faithful in tending to the little things that keep us moving forward, such as daily Bible reading, prayer, fellowship with other believers, and paying attention to our direction and priorities, we will become very effective in time.

The Lord spoke to a man in a vision some years back, and one of the things He said was this:

> *The darkness is growing and the time of great trouble will be upon you soon. If you do not use the time I give you, the coming troubles will overtake you. If you use the time I give you wisely,*

you will overcome and prevail. There is one characteristic com-
mon to the overcomers in every age—they did not waste their
time! [3]

There is a time for peace and a time for war. The Lord is not saying, "Fight all the time." But there will come times when we will have to choose to either fight or surrender, to either act or shut our eyes and hope it will turn out OK anyway. If we are in such a place and sense the Holy Spirit prompting us to persevere in prayer and faith, then *we are it.* God is handing us a mission. If we decide to not act, we are allowing the enemy an advantage that very possibly will make us and our families suffer consequences long after the incident has blown over.

With such a warning, some of us would jump on board and serve the King of kings out of sheer fear. But let us remember that we were set free by Christ to finally be able to choose that which leads to life—it is not a bondage to be under His orders, but increasing life and liberty. It is a privilege, not a burden. It is an opportunity to gain our inheritance in this life, to be free and be able to set others free, and to have victory over the things that were too strong for us. We have already been saved from our punishment—Jesus accomplished that on the cross. Now we have everything to gain by moving forward. The Lord does not force us to move with His commands. They are given for our sakes, to rescue us and to transform us into what we would truly love to become. They are there to help us overcome the voice of our enemy. The commands may seem stern or hard to understand, but we must recognize that He is always for us. The discipline especially is an expression of His love for us, not sparing us trouble when it will bring about long-term change and righteousness.

So then, with this in mind, the Lord *commands us* to be strong and fight, as spiritual children of Israel and partakers of His Kingdom. We are not to sit back and enjoy God's goodness without also striving to see His Kingdom come on earth (see Josh. 1:6-7;14-15; Hag. 1:2-4). Look at these Scriptures:

Son of man, I have made you a watchman for the house of Israel; so hear the word I speak and give them warning from Me. When you say to a wicked man, "You will surely die," and you do not warn him or speak out to dissuade him from his evil ways in order to save his life, that wicked man will die for his sin, and I will hold you accountable for his blood. But if you warn the wicked man and he does not turn from his wickedness or from his evil ways, he will die for his sin; but you will have saved yourself (Ezekiel 3:17-19).

If anyone would come after Me, he must deny himself and take up his cross and follow Me. For whoever wants to save his life will lose it, but whoever loses his life for Me and for the gospel will save it. What good is it for a man to gain the whole world, yet forfeit his soul? Or what can a man give in exchange for his soul? If anyone is ashamed of Me and My words in this adulterous and sinful generation, the Son of Man will be ashamed of him when He comes in His Father's glory with the holy angels (Mark 8:34-38).

We are entering into a time of increasing darkness. There will be waves of fear, despair, and lawlessness sweeping across the world, and we will be sent into all kinds of places to hold up the light of His mercy. In return for our love, we will be attacked on many levels, from those we come to help, from the passive bystanders, and even from our own Christian brothers and sisters who have fallen under the enemy's deception. We will face hardship; the question is, are we ready to overcome and keep serving?

God wants to train us as special troops. He wants people who are not afraid to advance against the gates of hell and disperse darkness with His light. As long as we keep moving forward, the light we carry and our swords and shields will keep us safe. But once we put our hand to the task, we must not go back (see Luke 9:62). We are called to fight through the canopy of lies, deception, and illusion that is heavy above and to loose the prisoners who march in the enemy's army (see 2 Cor. 10:4-5; Eph. 2:2; 6:12). The intimidation of the enemy will make him look large and his army undefeatable.

But we will keep winning as long as we stand firm (see Exod. 14:13-14; 2 Chron. 20:15-17; Isa. 7:9; 1 Cor. 16:13; James 5:8; Eph. 6:14). Let us press forward, and may the courage of the Lord be upon us!

PLEDGE OF ALLEGIANCE

At a specific point in time, we commit ourselves to something before the Lord, and He seals the vow. The commitment is binding on our lives, but as much as it hems us in, it also pushes us forward in our mortality to stand for His higher purposes.

Just as when a man and a woman make their vows of marriage, they commit to stay together. How many times since then have they been angry at each other or been tempted to throw in the towel and head for "easier" options. But the vow and respect for a promise keeps them working things through, leaving all of satan's tactics to separate them in the dust. The commitment to stay together was essential. Had it not been there, the couple would have left the door open for options.

We were saved and married to the Lord. Freely He gave Himself, and freely we stood before Him and took Him as our Lord. Come what may, we are committed to Him now. These last days are hard and will test our commitments to the core. There will be believers who have not trained themselves in perseverance, and they will fall. There will be believers who have never learned how to be dependent on the Holy Spirit, but on human leaders. They will be easily deceived. The Bible says many will fall away (see Matt. 24:10). But there will also be those who overcome. That is what we are training for. Our heart's desire must be to stay devoted to the Lord, to know His fellowship and His voice above all else, so that we will be able to run our race until the finish line.

Let me share a true story.

The Farao Islands in Northern Europe are islands riddled with witch-craft. A young man was saved despite this and went to preach the Gospel in South Asia. He had teamed up with another young man on fire for God, and they dared to stand on the open streets and preach in very dark areas of a Muslim country. When I met him, he told me that his background kept pushing him to such commitment.

"I have demons coming after me," he said. "One takes the shape of an old woman, and she keeps showing up in my room. Nasty looking woman. Once I was almost asleep when she came and stood by the bed. I was getting so used to her that I just took one look at her and said, 'Oh, it's you,' and turned around and went to sleep."

He was thoughtful, and then said, "There are generations of witchcraft behind me, and these demons hate that I have been set free by Jesus and am serving the Gospel. They want to kill me, but I am determined to run faster than them and to do as much damage as I can to keep them running."

The commitment to press forward kept this young man sane and constantly growing stronger spiritually, as he would not accept defeat.

We are entering an era of spiritual warfare as has never been before. Ours is the honor and responsibility to fight until the end, and many of God's warriors in previous ages would have given much to be with us now. Will you accept what the Lord calls you to do and share in the war and the glory?

I will never be the same again.
I can never return; I've closed the door.
I will walk the path; I'll run the race,
And I will never be the same again.[4]

PERSONAL REFLECTION

1. In what ways has the *unseen reality* become real to me?

2. How have I seen that there is a battle for my soul and over my life?

3. Have I accepted Jesus as my Savior and Commander of my life, or do I still play captain of my own life?

4. Do I want to join in the unseen battle to free myself and others from the power of satanic deception? Am I willing to learn what I need to know to become an effective soldier of Christ? Here is my commitment:

Signature: _____ Date: _____

ENDNOTES

1. Josh McDowell, *More Than a Carpenter* (Wheaton, IL: Living Books Tyndale, 1977), 25-34.

2. From the manual "Pastoral Care Ministry" (Omaha, NE: Trinity Church Interdenominational).

3. Rick Joyner, *The Call* (Fort Mill, SC: MorningStar Publications Inc., 2006), 41.

4. Geoff Bullock, "I Will Never Be the Same Again" (Word Music, 1996).

CHAPTER TWO

THE BATTLEGROUND I: DRAFTED

To help us understand the invisible world, we need to understand *who* is there. There are many in this realm who are for us and many who are against us. We will start our study with those who battle by our side, the Lord and His hosts.

MEET THE COMMANDER

Now when Joshua was near Jericho, he looked up and saw a man standing in front of him with a drawn sword in his hand. Joshua went up to him and asked, "Are you for us or for our enemies?" "Neither," he replied, "but as Commander of the army of the Lord I have now come." Then Joshua fell facedown to the ground in reverence, and asked him, "What message does my Lord have for his servant?"

The commander of the Lord's army replied, "Take off your sandals, for the place where you are standing is holy"... (Joshua 5:13-15).

When the Lord spoke to Moses from the burning bush, He told Moses to take off his shoes. Here it is again. Angels do not ask favors of respect from humans; they themselves are sent to serve the saints (see Rev. 22:7-9; Heb. 1:14). But a holy God will want all base things to be taken away from His presence.

This was no angel that met Joshua to prepare him for the battles ahead and to lead the way. The "Lord of the Armies" came out Himself. He is the Lord, the Most High, the King of kings. He is Jesus, a warrior and a hero from ancient days. He is not a puppet king who delegates the ugly wars to subordinates and then stays to watch at a safe distance. He Himself goes to battle.

Lift up your heads, O you gates; be lifted up, you ancient doors, that the King of glory may come in. Who is this King of glory? The Lord strong and mighty, the Lord mighty in battle (Psalm 24:7-8).

When the Jewish people thought of their Messiah, they were convinced that their coming king would be a man of war who would rescue their nation from all persecutors and bring final peace and prosperity into their unsettled times. They were not mistaken; they had read the Scriptures. Yet the Lord dealt with the greater issues first—their sinful hearts and their need for salvation. His second coming will not be as the first. The first visit secured His rightful ownership of the nations of the earth; the second visit will secure their obedience.

We may think of the Lord as the meek Lamb of God. Rightly so, for this is how He was revealed to us. But we are speeding toward the time of the Lord's second coming when He will come as King, not as a servant. He will come to rule. He will come to execute judgments on the earth. His coming will be so fearsome that people will run and hide in terror (see Rev. 6:15-17).

So, this is our Commander. He has never known defeat. He has never abandoned His soldiers. He knows no fear, and He is completely at peace and relaxed. He is a veteran warrior, and He is a superb and all-knowing strategist of war. If any circumstance scares us, it is because we are not keeping our eyes on the Commander. Fear melts away in His presence.

When we are in this army, we will soon realize that our Commander is very sensitive to His soldiers. We will never need to defend ourselves in front of anybody or try to prove our worth. If we are being wrongfully treated He promises to defend us in His own time and way. If we are suffering from being misunderstood among God's soldiers, we do not have to worry. He will promote us to our rightful place in due time. If we do the honorable thing when nobody is there to praise us, He sets aside a reward for later. He is immensely proud of our efforts, our diligence, our obedience, our faithfulness, and our perseverance (see Rom. 12:19; 1 Pet. 5:5-7; Matt. 6:1-4; Rev. 22:12; Matt. 25:21; Job 1:8; Ps. 149:4).

Oh yes, the Commander is tough. This is the army, you know. And He will be tough on *us!* Never to hurt us, to be sure, but to see that we get the training we need to succeed in war situations (see James 1:3-4; Ps. 18:32-36; John 15:1-2; Ps. 94:12-13). He will discipline us, too, if we start stepping over boundaries and breaking rules. He loves us enough to treat us like family—discipline, rewards, and all (see Prov. 3:11-12; Heb. 5:7-9; Rom. 8:17). He will do what it takes to get us ready for not only this life, but also for all the things He has planned for our eternal destiny.

We are completely safe with this Commander in charge, and yet most of His missions demand that our flesh-life dies. One man once said, "Help! Satan is out to kill me—and now I realize that God is, too!" Their motive is the opposite, though. Satan wants our destruction; God wants our resurrection. Therefore, the most painful war of our lifetime will still be worth the pain.

In this army, we have the great relief of not being in complete control of our own lives and destiny, nor that of our fellow soldiers or our family. It helps me to know as I get ready for warfare that:

- I am not in charge; He is.

- The battle is not mine; it is His.

- I do not assign myself my share of war; He does.

- The outcome of the war is not my responsibility; it is His.

- The ultimate safety of my family is not my responsibility; it is His.

- The ultimate safety of my body, soul, and spirit is not my concern; it is His.

- The outcome of the battle is not mine to judge; He alone is the Judge.

- My performance in the battle is not mine to evaluate; He alone knows the reasons for which He sent me and not someone else.

- Only this part is mine: to listen and to obey; the rest is His.

ANGELS

Now you have met the Commander. With Him are His servants, the angelic hosts. Thanks to many bad representations and misinformation, we need to spend a little bit of time to get a clear grasp on what angels are like and how they operate. They are on our team, and it is good to learn to count on them.

You may have seen pictures of naked baby cherubs shooting arrows from white, fluffy clouds. That is Greek mythology, not Christianity. It is also modern to view angels as female beauties with big wings, ministering protection to little children or bringing comfort. Although angels can show up in many human forms, we should not fall for the deception that angels are harmless and "nice."

Angels are not male or female in the way humans are. They are not made in God's image, but created to be His servants. They do not marry, and they cannot have "angel babies" (see Matt. 22:30). They are mostly mentioned in the masculine gender, and they often appear in the shape of a man.

Angels are immortal; they cannot be killed. They can be bound, and they win or lose battles (see Jude 6; Rev. 20:2; Luke 20:36). They were created in full number by God before He made the earth, and they neither increase nor decrease in number (see Job 38:4-7).

There are thousands of stories of people meeting angels who looked like normal people (some of them looking like motor bikers, old ladies, etc.), but who vanished inexplicably after helping a human in need.

Although angels are able to exercise a will of their own (which we see from satan's rebellion), they were created as servants, inclined to follow orders. There are several companies of angels, which are seen, for example, in the name "the Lord of hosts"—indicating more than one host. Jesus in Gethsemane commented that He could ask His Father for "twelve legions" of angels to come to His aid (see Matt. 26:53). The picture of companies becomes even clearer as we start looking at some angels mentioned to have authority over specific domains.

There are only a few angels mentioned by name in Scripture, which gives us the impression that they were of special authority. One such angel of great power was lucifer (who became satan, the archenemy of God). In his splendor and high position it is easy to see how he was able to draw such a following in the great rebellion. Michael the archangel is another powerful angel of high rank. He is the protector angel of the nation of Israel, and he will wage war against those demonic hordes that attack God's people (see Dan. 12:1). When there is war in the heavenlies, it is often between the fallen angels and the faithful angels who are guarding or attacking geographical areas or kingdoms. For example, when Daniel fasted for 21 days to understand a vision he had had, an angel was sent with an answer to him, but this angel was detained by "the prince of Persia." This principality had authority to rule the vast kingdom of Persia, and he was so strong that he hindered the angel from getting to Daniel for three weeks (see Dan. 10:13). Finally, Michael the archangel was sent to help in the battle so that the angel could deliver his message. This definitely gives us the impression that the angelic wars are very real and that the outcome depends on their number and strength.

Gabriel, the other famous angel, is the announcer. He heralded the coming of John the Baptist and Jesus Christ. The image we get from the activities of these named angels is that they have both different personalities and assignments. Michael is an angel of war. Gabriel is a favored messenger. Lucifer was an angel of wisdom and a steward of riches. With these high angelic commanders are the hosts of angels who serve the Lord. If we would ever meet such angels, we would quickly drop all notions of nice-looking guys with wings. These angels are warriors, big and fearsome (see Matt. 28:2-4). They are not "nice." If God tells them to protect you, they protect you. If God tells them to kill you, they kill you (see Ps. 78:43,49). They obey without reservation.

A friend of mine told me how she, before becoming a believer, had been out late one evening getting intoxicated with her friends. In the madness of the party turning sour, she had taken off on foot on the long and desolate road home. There was no traffic. At last a big truck on its way past stopped, and the large man inside looked her over and asked if she wanted a ride. She was about ready to climb in when she saw his eyes widen in terror, staring at something behind her. A strong light fell on his truck. The man revved his engine in panic and drove off as fast as he could. My friend turned around, but there was no one there. The light also had disappeared. She was standing alone again on the dark road. "That must have been one awesome, big angel! You should have seen that guy's face when he saw my protector!" she laughed as she told the story.

Most recorded incidents of people meeting angels show that the first natural response is to faint or become paralyzed with fear (see Luke 1:11-13; Dan. 10:4-11). This happened so frequently that angels learned that if they wanted to deliver a message they would first need to reassure the humans that they need not fear, but had actually been favored. Similar responses were also given when people encountered the Lord in His revealed glory (see Mark 9:2-6; Rev. 1:17). There is something so fearsome, so awe-inspiring about the Commander and His troops, when seen by the mortal eye, that He many times shades us from the full view. Instead He clothes Himself in human form and commands His angels to do the same so that they may serve without working havoc in our human existence.

The New Testament reveals that angels are servants of God's people (see Heb. 1:14). They are commanded to protect and shield believers from spiritual beings and attacks from the enemy. Psalm 91 is a psalm of divine protection on the man and woman who loves and follows the Lord. It states that if you seek your protection from the Lord, He will command His angels to guard you and see that you do not strike your foot against a stone (see Ps. 91:9-12). In the mid-1990s, as I served my first missionary term in South Asia, I was privileged to be under the spiritual guidance of an old native woman, Auntie Alice. When Alice, in her younger years, became a believer and received a calling as an evangelist, satan immediately counteroffered God's call by putting the position of head nurse with a fat salary in front of her. Fortunately, she saw through his attempt to sidetrack her and laughed. She became an evangelist and rejoiced in the fellowship of the Holy Spirit. One day many years later, as she was nearing her sixties, she was walking down a dusty road when satan decided to take her out for good. On a completely clear road, Alice suddenly stumbled on a "rock" that sent her into a back flip. She saw her death coming. Instead, she found herself unharmed, sitting on the road. No rock, no one around, and no injury. The vicious, demonic attempt on her life was intercepted by strong angelic protection.

Psalm 91 has become known as "The Soldier's Psalm," one that is often memorized by soldiers and prayed before combat. Through this psalm they lay hold of the promise that God will send angels to protect those who make Him their hope. The Veterans of Foreign Wars Post 2399 records the following:

> Almost 100 years ago, during World War I, the 91st Infantry Brigade of the US Expeditionary Army was preparing to enter combat in Europe. Because their commander was a devout Christian, he assembled his men and gave each of them a little card on which was printed the 91st Psalm, the same number psalm as their brigade. They agreed to recite that Psalm daily. After they had begun praying the Psalm, the 91st Brigade was engaged in three of the bloodiest battles of World War I—Chateau Thierry, Belle Wood and the Argonne. Other American units that fought in the same battles had up to 90 percent casualties, but the 91st Brigade did not suffer a single combat-related casualty.[1]

When my husband and I prepared ourselves to go overseas to a troubled part of the globe, we also started memorizing this psalm with our children. We felt we would need every bit of divine protection as we set foot on enemy soil. Numerous times we experienced relief from sickness, nightmares, fear, and security threats by simply saying this psalm together and trusting in His protection.

Angels take an interest in human affairs. They cannot comprehend all the aspects of salvation and God's dealings with humankind since they are created servants and not His children. There are things they are very curious about, and they rejoice when people are saved (see Luke 15:10). They are strongly inclined for worship and giving praise to the Creator, and they watch our worship with great interest. In fact, they realize that our worship is different and pleasing to the Lord in a special way so they clear the floor in front of Him and give us front row.[2]

Angels are *angels*; they are immortal, but they are servants, not "gods"— they are only in one place at a time, and they follow orders. Although satan fell with what could be one-third of Heaven's hosts,[3] there are still two-thirds faithfully at their posts. Although you only need the Lord on your side to be a majority in strength, it is still comforting to know that the ratio of angels is in our favor in a war situation (see 2 Kings 6:16-17). Do not fall under the illusion that there are just demons everywhere. The Lord's troops are greater, released at His commands. And very many times they are released to work in response to our prayers. It is not cowardly to ask the Lord to release angelic protection and help. It is prudent. Thank God for these serving spirits sent to help us win our battles.

POSITIONED

Now let us talk about how you and I fit into His army!

We have a place in the Lord's ranks. God saw our salvation before He made the world and way before He built our DNA! From ancient times He designed us to fit into His plan. His Word says that His plans for us are too numerous to count! (See Psalm 40:5; 139:17-18.) To fulfill these plans, He placed us strategically in the right time of history.

When we are with the Lord in eternity and outside the timeline and take a look at history, we will see ourselves fit in, and we will be in awe of the myriad of "clock-wheels" in motion—how everything worked together to accomplish His will. We will know the blessings we released through our obedience and how our simple actions put things in motion, and we will praise His wisdom.

To live in His plan is to find our place in His army. We do not have to be full-time ministers to be in His army; in fact, most of us are called to normal lives, but with the supernatural power of Jesus at work in our daily activities. The difference between us and those who live around us is that we live "under orders." Someone steers our lives, and we are increasingly moved to act according to His inner prompting. The fruit that proceeds from our lives will show that He initiated the action.

We advance or retreat according to His directions. The more we prove that we can take orders, the more He can use us. Many skilled people fall by the wayside of God's choosing because of their lack of listening. Many untrained, simple people advance to become generals by simply listening and executing orders swiftly (see Matt. 25:21).

Advancement in the heavenly realms comes through obedience and being tested. It does not matter how many talents, skills, and wonderful attributes we possess; we advance only through obedience. Jesus Himself learned obedience through the things He suffered (see Heb. 5:8-9), and that is what gave Him His inheritance of the nations from His Father. Every time we choose obedience and pass the test, we grow. We can spur our own growth rate by our willingness to submit to our times of training and testing.

Our specific place in His army is meant for us to fill, yet there is a warning. God will use somebody else, leave the task undone, or fill it Himself by people's prayers if we fail Him. We are important to Him, and He is gracious to wait for a season, but if we stop, God will still keep moving. Our calling is cemented and irrevocable in our lives (see Rom. 11:29), but there are a lot of little things He asks us to do that we need to be very swift to execute or they pass beyond our reach. If we sense that God is telling us to do something (especially when it comes to doing a good deed or asking forgiveness) it is better to err on the side of action than risk missing the opportunity. His gentle voice can be hard to distinguish, but the more we act on the promptings, the more we come to recognize His voice and become confident in our hearing.

A servant of God who worked in Africa found herself in a crisis one day. A person in the village had died, and she felt the prompting of the Holy Spirit to go and pray and raise him from the dead. She had never heard such a command before, and she was too timid to obey. Years later, she was still regretting her resistance to act, realizing that her disobedience cost the man his second chance to life and her own chance to declare the power of God.

Fortunately, the Lord usually trains us to hear His voice in smaller things first and in less dire circumstances. But even then the test is the same: Will we heed the voice of our Lord?

Let me share some good news now! Did you know that *nothing* that happens to us can remove us from our place in His army? Whatever He allows to happen to us, He already put into His plans, and it cannot move us. Death in the family, loss of a job, loss of respect, loss of health and beauty, loss of fortune—it cannot move us. There are only two things that can move us out of our position in the ranks: the Lord can change our position, or *we* can willfully step aside through disobedience. Unless we decide to ignore His orders, we are as firm as a rock in His plan. We may need healing; we may need understanding about why we are where we are at—but we are still soldiers, and we can still fight.

When we are in line with His plans, we receive authority to carry out all the things He places into our hands. This is called *positional authority.* If He tells us to lay our hands on someone, then we have the authority of the Most High to do so. If He tells us to go overseas, we go with His authority on our shoulders. If He tells us to pray, our prayers carry authority and are powerful. If He tells us to raise the dead, let us do it! If He tells us what He made us for, then we can confidently execute the authority of our office in His name. It is our portion, our assignment, and our honor from Him (see Ps. 16:5-6; 149). This is where we exercise the rod of authority—our sword—from Him.

Many of us are intimidated or scared at the prospect of doing these kinds of things, orders or no orders. We have a little commentator called "doubt" on our shoulder that keeps saying: "What if it does not happen? What if he does not get healed when I pray? I will look so foolish! What if He tells me to pray for rain and it does not happen? Then God's testimony will be ruined!" Well, tell little doubt to be quiet and listen.

We are not the ones who make miracles happen in the first place; God is. If He says, "Do it," then we do it. Many times we presume we know the outcome, when in fact we do not understand what He is doing. We just need to do our part and step aside. We place our trust in His goodness, whatever He decides to do. Presumption and disappointments can kill our faith, but if we simply do as we are told and let Him do His work—seen or unseen—we will not be damaged by what our eyes see. We can trust Him without having all the information. The Lord knows what He is doing.

Sometimes He sends His people on apparent "suicide missions" for their faith to test their level of stubborn obedience. A pastor once told us of his early years with the Lord. In a funeral service he suddenly felt the Lord telling him to pray for the dead body to be resurrected. He squirmed for a while under the pressure of the Holy Spirit, but then he took his place in the line to view the body. When he got there, he prayed for the dead body aloud—and nothing happened. Very embarrassed he left the building to fight it out with the Lord. But instead, the Lord told him, "I was testing you, to see if you would obey. Are you willing to be a fool for Me?" This time, the matter was not about a second chance for the dead, but to make a young man ready for ministry, obeying at whatever cost.

Many leaders and people who in these days carry enormous spiritual authority and see miracles happen started out with tests like these. Their trust in the Lord and their confidence in the fact that God is not capricious, but kind, were tested over and over while they kept obeying, waiting for the Lord to send His power. Let us not give up our confidence that God will act when we step out. His promise is that *"...he who seeks finds..."* (Matt. 7:8).

Finally, *let us not compare our position with anybody else's.* There is no valid comparison. We are all unique, and our missions are all unique. It is as ridiculous to compare our part in history as comparing athletes—one warming up for long-distance swimming, one in the middle of an intense 200-meter sprint, and a third going to the doctor to have his cast taken off after a sports accident. What is there to compare? We tend to get frustrated at others for neglecting what we see as the most important thing without realizing that it is important to *us* because it is our personal mission from the Lord. We need to set each other free from trying to do it our way; we are too specialized to be efficiently duplicated. Let us instead encourage each other as long as we run together so that we all may finish our tasks well (see Heb. 10:24-25).

THE TROOPS

So—there you are, enlisted in His army. And you are not a one-person strong army, either! Around you are thousands of other soldiers, standing in ranks, ready to serve beside you. Who are these? They are like you; they are believers in Jesus Christ who have abandoned a passive stance to their faith and have decided to advance His Kingdom. Jesus said, *"From the days of John the Baptist until now, the kingdom of heaven has been forcefully advancing, and forceful men lay hold of it"* (Matt. 11:12). These people beside you have, like you, decided to pick up their swords and become warriors for God's Kingdom.

This will quickly tell us that not all Christians are soldiers. There are "civilians," some because they are yet spiritual babies and youths who need to be nourished and trained, but sadly, there are also those who choose to remain civilians for their own sakes. All these depend on the army for their protection and nourishment. In case of war, they will not know what to do, and they will not be ready to fight. The Lord asks you to care for them (see Josh. 1:14-15).

There are also soldiers who are exempt from war for a season. The Lord wants them to care for their families and their inheritance and to enjoy their well-earned labor. You will see in God's instructions to the Israelite army that He set immediate family as a priority above service in war (see Deut. 20:5-8; 24:5). Therefore, if we see our family suffering because of our ministry or spiritual vocation, we must make the tough decision to take some time off and tend to our top task. This is not seen as retreat, but maintenance, and it has to get done. In fact, you show your worth by having your priorities straight (see Matt. 15:3-6; 1 Tim. 5:8). God will not punish you for withdrawing from a corporate fight if you notice your family needing your attention; He will honor you. When you have taken care of your household, you can step back in. Leave the battles with the Lord for a season; He can take care of them.

It is a common tactic of the enemy to attack the family unit rather than the ministry, thus destroying the servant's life and testimony as well. Let me be clear: to take time off of ministry opportunities is not the same as to stop serving in war. It is simply recognizing that your home is being infiltrated and needs to be jealously guarded by the head of the household. Reading numerous missionary biographies, my husband and I realized that in the early missionary movement of the 1800s and 1900s, the spiritual pioneers often sacrificed their families to serve the Lord. Many wives and children were left behind for the men to push forward; many children were sent far away to boarding schools; many women died of hardship or wilted for lack of attention from their husbands, who sacrificed *them* rather than themselves. The same scenarios are painted between the lines in Old Testament history: great men doing great exploits, but forgetting the home and the training of their children and caring for their wives. This is a slow and many times unnoticed snare on pioneers. The answer is not to push through at all costs "for the sake of Christ," but to guard and fight for the home ground. We can see this in the final hours of Jesus' life; He saw His mother Mary standing beneath the cross, and He made arrangements for His disciple John to care for her. He was not so wrapped up in His mission that He could not look to her needs (see John 19:26-27). When a house is built on a firm foundation, great ministries do not only flourish, but they also withstand the storms. A wonderful example of this is the William and Catherine Booth family. Both parents were involved in starting the Salvation Army, but they were also intensely guarding, loving, and training their eight children at home. The fruit became evident as all their children decided to serve the Lord later on.[4]

Let us return to our position in the army and talk about *soldier interaction.* We have a whole bunch of friends waiting to be discovered. Some of them will be "higher" than us in rank, some lower. Some will have huge responsibilities; some are free to come and go, doing one thing at a time. Some are incredibly talented, while others serve in humble maintenance. The thing to remember is that *we are all on the same team.* We will be glad for others' strength, wit, and skills when we are in the heat of battle.

In the army there is no room for jealousy, competition, or comparison. It could destroy our relationships and ruin our service. Our task is to be the best we can for our specific task so that we will bless many. We will all be rewarded according to what we have been given to care for (see Matt. 25:14-30).

Did I just mention that we are on the same team? That implies that his or her victory is ultimately your victory! When a battle is won, all soldiers involved rejoice and are rewarded. This is something I had to learn as a wife. I saw my husband have a chance to go somewhere to preach or through his job impact the work world. He came and went while I stayed home with our children. Many times I was jealous of his role, and I had to remind myself that I served as back-up for him, praying and covering the home grounds while he was away. But the principle in the Lord's army is, that *the one who cares for the soldiers' supplies and family and who grants support in different measures is equal to the one who goes to war, and he receives an equal share in the booty of the battle* (see 1 Sam. 30:23-25). Whether we are on the frontline waging war or serving behind the scenes through prayer or support, we all are rewarded for doing what we are asked to do.

There is no room for "God's lone rangers" who stay apart from the army. We are sent out *from* the army, and certainly should not take on the hordes of darkness by ourselves. If you tried it once, you may be one of those civilians now. To try to take on the enemy horde single handedly is absolutely foolish. We need the covering and protection that comes from being part of the army that moves at His orders. In God's camp there is only one Hero, and that is the Commander Himself. He has the reputation of having taken down the whole enemy camp once in a single blow! You may dream of being a John Wayne or a Zorro for God, but you better not look for opportunities to try it out! There are scores of "little heroes" in our midst, but they are suspiciously looking like normal soldiers who "Just did my duty, Sir. Glad to serve You, Sir!"

We are all directly under the authority of the Commander. Even if we take orders from sub-commanders, we are held responsible to follow the given codes of conduct, the Scriptures.

Every soldier's conduct will be appropriately commended or disciplined by the Commander. If we have seniority status and see blatant sins, we may be assigned to correct a fellow soldier. But the general rule in this army is encouragement, not judgment (see Luke 6:37-38). Our motto for soldier to soldier attitude is: *encouragement, humility, love, and service* (see Heb. 10:24-25; Phil. 2:3-4; John 15:12-14; Matt. 20:25-28).

We are to help each other forward. The war, the battle, the snares, and our own weaknesses are enough to put us down; we desperately need to be affirmed by others alongside us, not criticized. God is more than able to correct all things, from the worst offenses to the minutest misalignments. He is also a great deal more gentle and accurate than we are. He is definitely impartial and always has all the facts. Avoid dishing out criticism; promote unity.

If you are sent on a group mission, the team's health and life will dictate its ability to succeed. *You can only go as fast as your slowest member,* so everyone has to back and support the weakest. The enemy will always target the weakest member or the weakest area of a team to try to break the advancement or dissolve the unity.

Many of God's teams end up with a number of strong-willed people—their determination to push forward was the very thing that helped them get on the team in the first place. This too can become an effective way for the enemy to start power struggles in our midst when we were meant to have incredible thrust forward through our combined strengths.

Lastly, the Lord requires purity in His soldiers. In the Old Testament times the Lord commanded the soldiers to keep their camp separated from impurities (see Deut. 23:9). In the same way we need to be careful that we do not despise the Lord's presence when we go to war. It might be very humbling to repent in front of people, but if that is what it takes to release the Lord's power, then let us do it. Let us serve our great Commander with clean hands and a pure heart and give no advantage to the enemy. The Lord reigns in our midst!

THE LOST

Now you have been introduced to your Commander, the heavenly armies of the Lord, your allies, and your own place as a soldier. We will soon move over to look at the other side of the battlefield, where your enemy dwells and prepares his attacks. He has armies, too, hordes of them. But in his dark territory are also multitudes of people who have no idea of where they are, what they are doing, and how to ever get out of their situation to find light. They are in his domain, they are influenced by his doctrine, but not all of them have sworn him allegiance. Some of them are just lost in the dark.

Derek Prince once shared the story of how he was on a train ride in a foreign country. As the train slowed down for a station, he looked out the window and watched the crowd and the shuffle outside. As he looked at the people milling around, he wondered to himself, "I wonder how God sees those people." He was startled when the Lord suddenly answered. *"Some weak, some foolish, some proud, some wicked, some exceedingly precious."*[5]

If this is how God views people, then we may view them this way as well. Not everybody we meet will be receptive to the good news of Jesus, but some will. Some will have a desire for what is good; some will be lusting for wickedness. Some will live simple lives without reaching out for God, never stopping to reflect that there is someone who they one day will have to give an account to. Some will not come to Him because of sin and rebellion and some because of pride. But among the lost are also the "exceedingly precious" people, those who cannot stop hoping and seeking for God and who cry out for help.

These are all in the dark domain. They are prisoners unawares. They cannot leave their domain—they are bound with fetters and chains and are wearing eye-patches to hinder them from seeing their own situation. Generational curses are binding some; others have succumbed to being slaves to their sinful passions. Some have consciously or unconsciously sworn allegiance to demons, while others are just oblivious to the spiritual reality and are trying to "make the best" of their lives. But all of them are in satan's realm and captives until they turn to Christ.

One of the universal missions the Lord has given His soldiers is to rescue those who want to be rescued from the domain of darkness. He wants the invitation to go out to all the prisoners to let all of them know there is a way out (see Matt. 24:14). But the mission is not to rescue all; it is to find and rescue the "exceeding precious" ones. Do not take this wrong; they *could* all be saved, if they chose to. The tragic thing is that those who are accustomed to darkness start being comfortable with it, and they do not want to be rescued; they enjoy their sin too much.

To be put on this rescue mission will break your heart time and again. It breaks God's heart, too. But when you are discouraged, remember the precious ones. They are there. They are waiting for answers and to know that God sees them. They are waiting for the rescue crew, beyond reason or hope. If you meet the weak, the foolish, the proud, and the wicked ones— do not give up. Keep holding your lamp up in dark places and search for the exceedingly precious ones. If you see even one of them saved, you will enter the joy of your King.

Personal Reflection

1. How do I recognize the voice of my Commander? What could I do to strengthen my ability to hear Him?

2. Do I know what my role in the army is (in other words, do I know what God wants me to do long term or short term with my life and what level of authority I can exercise to see it done)?

3. Am I in the place God wants me to be? Have I followed His directions up to this point, or is there something I am avoiding or procrastinating in?

4. Who do I have around me whom I think God placed there to be my fellow soldier, to encourage, challenge, and help me? Am I paying attention to what they are teaching me (in word or in action)?

ENDNOTES

1. "The Soldier's Psalm," *Veterans of Foreign Wars Post 2399*, http://vfwpost2399.org/psalm91.aspx (accessed June 17, 2010).

2. The Lord let me see this one time during worship. The angels just stepped aside to let us come to the front, to give us a large space to minster before Him.

3. Revelation 8:12 and 12:1 speak of a third of the stars falling to the earth. Stars many times symbolize angels in Scriptures.

4. William Booth, *Training Your Children for Christ* (Last Days Ministries, Pretty Good Printing, 1985).

5. Derek Prince (1915–2003), audio message, "Take Heed to Yourselves." Information about Derek Prince is available at http://www.derekprince.info/Groups/105988/DPM/About_Derek_Prince/About_Derek_Prince.aspx.

CHAPTER THREE

THE BATTLEGROUND II: ENEMY CAMP

MASTER OF DECEIT

N ow we are going to take a look at our enemy. In no way do I think it is healthy to dwell on satan, as he loves to get such attention and to inspire fear. But we will look at him from the standpoint of warfare, to know what we are up against. *Do we know where he comes from? Is he limitless? Could he win? Does he have any weaknesses? Who are with him, and how many are they? What is it they want? What are they afraid of?*

We know quite a bit about satan's origin and what he is after. A major insight can be gained from studying Ezekiel 28:12-19 and Isaiah 14:12-20. Although the first layer of these prophetic texts concerns historic kings, we quickly find out that the Lord is talking about an enemy of His that walked the heavenlies.

As we study these Scriptures we can draw a number of inferences. Satan, at the start, was created good and was the most beautiful of all angels. He was wise as well. On the very same day God made this angel, He also created riches. All this heavenly and earthly wealth—everything that to this day has not lost its value, such as gems and gold—was given to this beautiful angel for him to be guardian of. And his headquarters? Eden, Earth.

It appears to me that when God creates a living being, He lays down in him a desire for the very thing He plans for him to work with. For us humans, this is definitely the case. When we find our life work, we tend to say, "I was made for this." We know that we have found our place. God planted in lucifer the desire for riches. And as the steward, he started trading with these riches, and he found that he gained power through them.

This trading led to his demise. He could not resist trying to gain more than he gave. His great wisdom aided him now in his attempt to beguile his fellow angels and yet keep their trust. His unearthly beauty and leadership intoxicated him to desire more all the time. After he had been given all the greatest riches of Heaven and a great position of honor among the angels, he still lusted for more. More power, more glory. The admiration of the other angels was not enough. He wanted their utter devotion. He desired to be their god. No, more than that, he desired *to be God Himself, the ruler of all.*

When violence and pride had filled lucifer's heart, God removed his guardianship of the heavenly riches and threw him to earth. With him came those angels he had won over, a third of Heaven's host.[1] He went straight to the garden and to his headquarters. He was still beautiful, still wise—but fallen and corrupt. His pride was hurt by his heavenly demotion, and he was jealous of God's new creation—humanity. Lucifer was beautiful, but he was not created to be like God. But these *people*...created in God's image! What satan coveted he could not get, and these mortal beings received it without even knowing what they had! There were only two options in his mind for humankind: They could either accept him as their god or be destroyed. His obsession ever since has been to steal from God whatever is precious to Him and to make himself so powerful that he can attain his goal of godhood.

Satan is no god and never will be. He is a fallen angel of great powers, great beauty, and great intellect, but he is still just an angel. If you have heard of yin and yang, the Asian view of god, then you will have heard it said that evil and good are equally strong and neither of them can win. This is something satan would gladly want you to believe, but it is far from the truth. He is a banished rebel from the heavenly realms with a death sentence hanging over him, and the clock is ticking. He is hellishly clever and deceitful, but he is not infinite. He cannot be in all places at the same time, and he does not fill all things like God does (see Job 1:6-7). Even though he knows Scripture and can quote portions to you, he fears his own doom and has deceived himself to think that he has a chance to win God's throne before his time is up. He exercises a tremendous influence and has gained a large following, but he is not all-powerful.

Satan has the same personality make-up that God gave him from the beginning, although, like us, it is marred by sin and rebellion. He is forever attracted to riches, and much of the worldly riches have been channeled to serve his intentions. Though it is true that *the earth is the Lord's, and everything in it* (Ps. 24:1), the Lord does not exercise His right as the Creator over this planet through control, but through love, until the appointed time of His rule with the iron scepter (which is the reign of Christ during the Millennial Kingdom). Even then, the basis of judgment will be from the way we have responded to His love shown in the sacrifice of Jesus, as Father God lays all things under His feet (see 1 Cor. 15:27-28).

In the meantime, satan is very active in trying to win as much terrain and as many followers as he possibly can. When Jesus came and was tested in the desert, satan implied that he, satan, was the ruler of—and accessed the riches of—all the kingdoms of the world. He knew that Jesus would desire to have them as the rightful heir. There is need for a clear perspective here. First John 5:19 says that *"...the whole world is under the control of the evil one."* He exercises authority over the world system and in the skies above the individuals and nations that have not submitted to the lordship of Christ. Yet we must also remember that satan is a defeated enemy on a divine leash, as long or as short as the Lord determines. He may be on a longer leash for the moment, but only so that God can test the hearts of people. In his pride, he constantly deceives himself about his own status and prospects. He may still disguise himself as an *angel of light*, but there is no light in him (see 2 Cor. 11:14).

It is interesting to me that, when in the sixth century Muhammad saw visions of an angel, the angel introduced himself as Gabriel to verify his authority. I do not believe Muhammad was a lunatic or that he made this up. From these visions the religion of Islam has sprung up, and to this day it shows tremendous spiritual resistance to the Gospel of Christ. Lucifer, the "angel of light," having held such a high rank among the angels, could easily have put on his glow again. He is the father of lies. Islam did not originate in the mind of a man, but with this deceiver. It carries his violence, his arrogance, and his hatred toward God's people, both physical Israel and Christians. Islam acknowledges just enough biblical truth to make it almost immune against the power of the Gospel to save. It is strong to this day because people submit themselves to its lordship five times a day.

After looking at lucifer's beginning, as well as his personal attributes, I would like to point out what his position is in reference to us, the Lord's people. Of all the information on warfare that could be gathered, this is one of the absolute most crucial ones to understand and have imbedded in our attitude. It is simply this: *satan has already been defeated.* There is no question of how the great war of the ages is going to turn out. Satan was defeated by Christ on the cross once and for all, when he was stripped of his powerful allies *sin* and *death.* They were his primary weapons against Adam's race, and Jesus, the second Adam, defeated them by fulfilling their rightful claims through his death. While in the grave, He preached the good news of forgiveness to those already dead and so robbed death of its prisoners. As He rose, His victory over death was completed, and He paraded His victory over all His enemies through the heavenlies, showing off His booty. You can read about this in Ephesians 4:8-10 and Colossians 2:13-15.

It was a day of utter humiliation for satan and all his followers, and believe me, they do remember that day! As much as they do not want to be reminded of it, they also would like all Christ's followers to be ignorant of their complete defeat. But you and I must not forget, for Christ's victory is our glory and our confidence in the face of all that confronts us in life. His victory was *for us*, and it has become our victory! We may falter or fall; we may be weak in our service; we may be discouraged or accused by our adversary—but the truth still stands![2] We can raise our heads and point to Jesus and say: "Do you see Him, satan? Do you remember that day when He stripped you of your weapons? And I, by the grace of my Lord, have a place in the victory procession—not because of me, but because of Him! What charge will you bring that can prevail against the Blood of Jesus, shed for me?"

Despite satan's defeat, the Lord is allowing him to be on the loose until the time is fulfilled. Although hateful and evil, his havoc among people serves the Lord's twofold purpose of testing hearts and refining His people. Only fire brings out pure gold. The terror and destruction we see now are not going to have the last say! The Lord was the one who threw lucifer to earth in ancient times; He is the one who will soon throw him into his final prison, eternal hell (see Matt. 25:41; Rev. 20:7-10). And *we*—we can rest assured, for we will see it done.

PRINCIPALITIES

For our struggle is not against flesh and blood, but against rulers, against authorities, against the powers of this dark world and against the spiritual forces of evil in the heavenly realms (Ephesians 6:12).

Satan is not alone. He emptied Heaven of a third of its immortal inhabitants. Even fallen angels are mighty beings, fearsome, strong, and impossible to kill. They can be restrained, though. Until their final destination in the lake of fire, the people of God are to resist their work, overthrow their rule, forbid them entry into our realm of authority, and bind them, thus hindering their activity. The Lord has given His followers the authority to "bind" and "loose" (see Matt. 16:19). When we are confronted with demonic forces, this is something we need to be prepared to do as the Holy Spirit prompts.

We should never see human beings as our enemies. They can give their strength to serve satan, and they are the hands and feet to do his work. Yet, the Lord did not prepare hell for humans. It was prepared for satan and those angels who rebelled with him (see Matt. 25:41). It was not intended for God's image-bearers to have to taste the eternal fire; they were destined for glory. However evil men and women become, they are not the source of the problem. They are deceived, manipulated, blinded, and coerced. They are to be pitied, not hated, for their end will be terrible as they share the fate of demons.

Your battle is in the unseen realms. The Scriptures do not say that the battle is against one generic group of corrupted angels. In fact, they are quite different from each other, as we can see from Ephesians 6:12; the Word describes them as *rulers, authorities, powers of this dark world, and spiritual forces of evil in the heavenly realms*—different, distinct categories of opposition.

From the words *spiritual forces of evil in the heavenly realms* we get the idea that demonic activities take place in spiritual realms different than both our physical earth and God's Heaven. Principalities are rulers who exercise authority and influence over major geographical areas, people groups, and cultures and who war against the hosts of the Lord who keep pressing them in response to human prayer (see Dan. 10:12-14). As we will study later, there are many other demonic forces that serve these principalities, but do not have the same authority. Often these smaller demons are referred to as "evil spirits" rather than rulers, and they seek to control individuals or families. They are the ones we command rather than war against, as we do with principalities.

The principalities are the ones who put layer after layer of deception and illusion in the air, turning the skies to bronze.[3] They gain strength through human sin and cooperation, which ignores the mercy of God.[4]

These principalities are not faceless clones. They have names—*descriptive* names that reveal their operations and intentions. An example is from the book of Daniel, where we find a high-ranking principality called "the prince of Persia." As his title describes, he was the authority of spiritual wickedness and influence over a vast empire. The archangel Michael had to fight him in order for one of God's angels to come through his domain (see Dan. 10:13). There are other demonic powers mentioned in Scripture. Revelation 9:11 mentions "apollyon," which in Greek means "destroyer." Another demon is simply named "death"—it makes us realize that death is not a state, but a *being!* (See Revelation 6:8.)

Scriptures reveal that many feelings we succumb to are actually spiritual influences in whose atmosphere we have entered; thus, they are called a "spirit of fear" or "a spirit of despair." There are levels of strength here as well—they can affect an individual who has succumbed to deception, but they can also affect a whole region.[5] We can start distinguishing these from our natural feelings by their sudden presence where earlier we had no such thoughts or feelings at all. When such discernment is practiced and understood, we would call this the gift of discernment of spirits. It is a gift greatly to be desired by His soldiers.

If this sounds strange to you, I would like to give you some examples. It may well be, as you read this, that you start recognizing demonic activity around you. Although uncomfortable to be aware of, it does help you know how to pray and stand.

In Sweden, my sister came with a group of believers to a New Age convention to pray and to seek out needy people. The place was rank with evil! The atmosphere was so heavy that they had to go outside the tent for air. The people inside, who did not have the inner testimony of the Holy Spirit, did not notice.

When my husband as a young man traveled across the border from a Muslim country into Hindu territory, he later described it as walking through a veil; the oppression that he had lived under for months lifted the moment he stepped out of Islamic territory. I do not say that the Hindu region was any cleaner spiritually, but it is often that we notice a shift in the pressure above.

Sensitive people are many times acutely aware of any change in the atmosphere they are in. This is most obvious when traveling; they can get so weary from the new spiritual pressure that they get sick. An acquaintance of ours shared how he had worked in the city of Kandahar, Afghanistan, for six months. The whole team had unanimously decided to have devotions and to worship every evening, mainly to be able to stay healthy in the darkness of the city—Kandahar is one of the high seats of fundamental Islamic leadership and propaganda.

Another man was serving the Lord by praying and seeing geographical land redeemed from curses. While visiting a new country and region he had been praying for, he started having acute chest pains when he crossed over a significant spiritual border. Those he traveled with confirmed that the place was spiritually significant.

My husband is at the moment on assignment from the Lord to pray against a certain spirit in our region. He realized some months back that his headaches were a sign that this spirit was being active somewhere in the city. Thus, the Lord has given him a way to feel out the enemy and be able to divert his plans through prayer before it has a chance to bring its human participant into full criminal action.

Many names have been revealed of principalities and small rank demons through counseling and exorcism these past decades. Have you for example heard of "Jezebel?" The historical figure was a wicked queen in the Old Testament, a practitioner and priestess of the occult and the actual ruler of Israel through her weak-minded husband Ahab.[6] Her hatred was toward Elijah the prophet, who spoke out about her wickedness. In these days, the name jezebel is circulating again as the name of a principality. One of the characteristic marks of the jezebel spirit influencing an individual, a group, or even a church or ministry will be manipulative control, domination, and a quenching of the prophetic voice. The principality is the force and the influence of wickedness; the serving demonic hordes are those who do the "foot work." Many of them, as has come out in counseling sessions, have names that identify their primary purposes: "control," "manipulation," "lust for power," "domination," and so forth.

There is a principality that the Lord has revealed to be constantine, the spirit of organized religion. Historically, from the time of the first martyrs and up to modern day, the trend has been as follows:

1. Gospel proclamation in a dark land

2. The beginning of a church

3. Violent persecution or opposition

4. A time of mercy and the growth of the church

5. An acceptance of Christianity in the country's government

6. The establishment of the church institution

7. Regulated and organized church functions and traditions

8. The church slowly falling asleep in its comfort

9. The fire of the Holy Spirit neglected and smothered

This is not how it is supposed to develop! This is the work of a smart enemy who knows the religious souls of people all too well. If he cannot kill instantly, he will go and drain the life out of a fellowship slowly and covertly through a steady "blanketing" of the skies. Demons move into the void of the absence of the Holy Spirit; where He is not allowed lordship, the rulers of the earth (humankind) are giving darkness permission to enter. If you consistently go home from church as empty as you came and cannot feel the move of the Holy Spirit and see no evidence of God showing up and find the sermon dealing with technical theology rather than bringing life and spiritual growth—then your church may have fallen into enemy hands. The Lord alone knows the whole situation about the condition of our churches; we need to seek His will about any move we make. But it would be wise to go and search for air before you faint. You will not have the strength to fulfill your calling from the Lord unless your spirit is properly fed.

Finally, let us talk about what we can do against these principalities! They are not the kind that you sternly command and they submit. They are the kind that the Lord's angels do not rebuke, but war against (see Rev. 12:7-9). When it comes to evil spirits and the kind that indwell people and animals, which we will talk about soon, you can name them and drive them out. But when you find out what principality is working in your area, you need to band together—the more believers and warriors, the better. These are some practical steps a church or a city or a committed troop can take to change the spiritual atmosphere in an area:

1. Repentance—personal and on behalf of those in the area. Check that your heart is pure so that the enemy has no entry in you.

2. Fasting and prolonged times of prayer, especially seeking the Lord for discernment and strategy for breakthrough.

3. Worship watches with the intent of building a platform from which His authority can extend. Darkness cannot overcome light, but light drives out darkness!

4. Gathering information: research the place for historically significant happenings (see the section titled "Researching History"), and couple this information with revelation from the Holy Spirit through dreams and prophetic words and pictures. Look for root causes that could have given the principality entry (it always finds its way through human activity, such as a curse, unforgiveness, bloodshed, witchcraft, and so forth).

5. Standing your ground. To worship in a dark place is energy-consuming, but once you have planted your feet through worship, you will remove evil without being moved yourself.

6. Intentional and well-prepared attack forward. When the Lord has revealed what you as a team are up against and shown you the strategy in how to deal with it,[7] then stand on the authority you know you have received and declare the downfall of your enemy. Often this process involves personal and corporate repentance and repenting on behalf of the area. It may take a number of times, weeks, or months for a principality to move. It may have had many entries. You bar one door, but he still has access to others. Keep asking the Lord for revelation and strategy, and He will keep handing you the information you need. This is war, not a one-time combat; it will take time and perseverance to break through. But if you stay at it to the end, I promise you, your name will be circulated in unseen camps. Next time they will fear your resolve and give up faster than this time around.

It is my experience that the Lord Himself will close the chapter on a specific war. He will let you know when it has all been dealt with—otherwise, we would not know if there were more things that needed to be addressed. On a personal level, the Lord brought me through two such times of repentance and deliverance, and both times He sealed those seasons with promises at the end, letting me know that all had been taken care of.

On a corporate level, you should see radical changes take place! The removal of a demonic principality, coupled with the fervent prayers of the saints, will open an area and its people for a move of God and the harvesting of souls. I want to give as example the transformation process the Lord brought the Umuofai people of Nigeria through as they started repenting of their occult and wicked practices.

When some of the people first responded to the Gospel in a meeting, the Holy Spirit descended and guided them through a series of steps in getting rid of generations of spiritual idolatry. The leaders of the people brought their sacred items forward. Then the families entered a time of personal repentance toward each other and under deep conviction.

The Holy Spirit then told the people to renounce all the covenants they had made with spirits for the last 300 years. When this was finally done, the Lord told the people to go and deal with their shrines. The leaders again led the way, breaking all agreements made with spirits generations ago. The people brought their personal fetishes from their homes and set them on fire.

By the time they had done this, they had been together in repentance and strategic warfare for over nine hours. When it was over, the village experienced something like a revival celebration; the Lord had dealt with all their wicked ways, and they were free to dance in their newfound freedom![8]

THE MARK OF IDENTIFICATION

To help us in our understanding of the demonic world and how it operates, we will need to study some aspects of what names represent in the spiritual realm. The more I study names and meanings, the more I realize that there is much more to a name than just something that we are called by. *A name is a mark of identification.* Just like an identification badge, it will not only tell who the bearer is, but also who the owner is.

This is vividly portrayed in the New Testament and especially in the book of Revelation. We find that the Lord calls us by His own name and that He will place the mark of His name on our foreheads (see Rev. 3:12; 14:1; 22:4). We are His own, His family. We bear His name.

In a similar fashion, satan will in the last days enforce a mark on the foreheads of all humankind, *a mark that is his name* (see Rev. 13:16-17). It might be easy to fall into the trap of thinking that we can take the mark yet secretly belong to the Lord. We must realize that we identify ourselves with the one whose mark we bear—it becomes who we are. The Lord was very clear that we must be willing to identify ourselves with Him before people if we want Him to acknowledge us in the courts of Heaven (see Luke 12:8-10).

The Jewish leaders in Jesus' time knew that names were powerful. When they arrested the disciples, their first action was always to order them not to speak in the name of Jesus. They asked them, *"By what power or by what name did you do this* [healing]*?"* (Acts 4:7). They knew that the authority of the person whom the name represented had been released and had caused the miracle.

Although we might not recognize the power of names, it is still there since names are spiritual identification marks. I think most of us have had experiences in this, though we might not have understood it. A father, a mother, a teacher, or some other person exercising influence over us spoke a name or an identity into us for good or for evil. "My beautiful princess"—valued, blessed, favored. "You lazy, good-for-nothing son"—devalued and cursed! The father just threw an identity on his son that he will not be able to lift off by his own power. Unless he is released, he will start acting in the nature of this identification. Nicknames—some are pleasant, but many are so destructive. *If we agree with them*, we have actually pinned them to our identity badge and made them part of our name. If some acquaintance would then come and say some encouraging word in opposition to this name, we would compare it to our accepted name and then throw the encouragement out, even if it was the truth. It did not match up with our identity.

When we are saved, the Lord is the one who frees us from old identification marks and gives us a new identity. He can do this because He is our new owner, our true Father. When He speaks over us, we can let the old things go and put on our new name, our new identity. *"Though all the peoples walk each in the name* [identity] *of his god, as for us, we will walk in the name of the Lord our God forever and ever"* (Micah 4:5 NASB).

This understanding of names helps us resist demonic attacks and infiltration. They find their best opportunities in darkness, where they are not seen. Once they are identified as servants of the evil one, there is no more deception to hide behind, and they must obey the authority that flows from the name of Jesus—remember, we bear His name, so we are identified as His. Therefore, the demons have no legal right to harass us. They stole in the back door as thieves in the cover of night (ignorance or deception), and they are ordered out (in the authority of Jesus, the rightful owner) when they are discovered in the daylight (revelation and identification).

Evil Spirits and the Power of Agreement

We have already mentioned the difference between principalities and evil spirits. Principalities control the air; evil spirits desire to inhabit a person or an animal.

I think we in the West have so successfully learned to disregard the spiritual reality that we have given our enemy a great advantage and too much room to maneuver. Rather than realizing spirits at work around us, we identify the thoughts and feelings that arise in us as our own and do not understand to fight the invasions on our beings. Ignorance makes us easy victims to demonic deception (see Hos. 4:6). We need to become alert to the thoughts that enter our minds.

> *The weapons we fight with are not the weapons of the world. On the contrary, they have divine power to demolish strongholds. We demolish arguments and every pretension that sets itself up against the knowledge of God, and we take captive every thought to make it obedient to Christ* (2 Corinthians 10:4-5).

There is power in agreement. There is power when we agree with people or demons, and there is power when we agree with the Lord. The Lord loves unity so much among His people that He has promised to answer our prayers if we can just get one other believer to agree with us before His throne (see Matt. 18:19).

There are spiritual laws in effect that are as sure and effective as the natural laws of our universe. When the Lord made mankind to be caretakers of planet Earth, He gave us great authority and influence over our domain. What we speak and declare—whether good or evil—goes. When we agree with anyone, the spiritual laws uphold the agreement. The Lord will not break off the thoughtless or harmful agreements we have made with demons, but He wants to train us to become wise and learn how to *take responsibility* for the words we say, *break all evil agreements* we have made in the past, and recognize and *fight all new invasions* on our minds (see James 3:6-10).

We can see that the primary weapon of the Lord's ministry on the earth was the spoken word. It was how He defeated the temptations in the desert trial (see Matt. 4:1-11) and sent satan away. He also taught His disciples to command the evil spirits when He trained them for ministry (see Matt. 10:8). *Our strength is in agreeing with God and resisting the lies of the devil.*

Much of our successful confrontation with the demonic will spring from this basic understanding of agreement. On the personal level, we battle to submit our minds to agree with the Word of God and to break old habits of agreeing with our enemy about ourselves and our condition. Unless we submit ourselves to obeying the Word of God, for example in forgiving another's sins against us, we will then find ourselves captured by a spirit of unforgiveness and being used against the Lord's people.

When we battle for other people, the principles are the same. In counseling the main focus is finding the roots that have opened the door to unhealthy thoughts or behaviors (spiritual, emotional, or physical) so that the agreements made in the past can be broken.

I want to make this practical for you now. For some of you, the very thought of naming evil spirits and commanding them to leave may be foreign or even scary. Is it necessary to personify anger, lust, unforgiveness, jealousy, and so forth? How can we tell the difference between, for example, being angry and being under the influence of a spirit of anger?

First of all, let us realize that being under the influence of a spirit is a common state for humankind—the question is, *what* spirit are we influenced by? One of the most wonderful things in life is to feel the Spirit of God descend on us and fill us with His life. All born-again believers can testify to periods of time when they were under the influence (control) of the Holy Spirit—He took over, giving great peace or overwhelming joy or divine grace. It was not *you* that changed—it was *Him* manifesting in your mortal body! You were under the influence of a Spirit!

Humans are likewise desirable homes to demons. Their first intent is always to try to *indwell and control* a human body. If the Holy Spirit has made us His home, then He will not allow this intrusion. The Holy Spirit is our safeguard against what we call *demon possession.*

Demons seek empty homes that have doors open. The doors are the entry ways to our beings. If we agree with darkness we open the door for darkness to enter. For example, if we yield ourselves to nurse our anger rather than letting it go, we are opening a door for a spirit of anger to come and master us, letting it feed on our emotions and our unwillingness to forgive. While we were initially the ones choosing to be angry, the spirit of anger will soon be strong enough to control *us.* A person thus controlled will be driven to act according to that spirit and will feel it take over in certain situations. He will feel overwhelmed, overcome, and driven to do things that he would normally not do.

For born-again believers, we may not have to deal with being possessed by a demon, but we can still be *harassed and steered by spirits* who attach to us from the outside. By *harassing spirits,* I mean evil spirits that follow us around to whisper, entice, and torment our minds to hinder our service. If they find no door open in us, then that is all they can do. We dismiss the thoughts and give them no chance to sprout in our hearts.

If there are doors open in a believer's heart (such as unforgiveness, lust, or lying), a demon is able to get enough of a grip to ride him. Sharing a vision from the Lord of the end-time battles, Rick Joyner writes in his book *The Final Quest* the following about the enemy army:

> The most shocking part of this vision was that this horde was not riding on horses, but primarily on Christians!…While these people professed Christian truths in order to appease their consciences, they lived their lives in agreement with the powers of darkness. As they agreed with these powers,

their assigned demons grew and more easily directed their action...

I noted that the demons were riding on these Christians, but were not in them as was the case with non-Christians. It was obvious that these believers had only to stop agreeing with their demons in order to get free of them...

The power of the demons was clearly rooted almost entirely in the power of deception, but they had deceived these Christians to the point where they could use them and the Christians would think they were being used of God. This was because banners of Self-Righteousness were being carried by almost everyone, so that those marching could not see the banners that marked the true nature of these divisions...[9]

Again we see that the warfare against such intruders comes from breaking our agreements with their lies and turning to speak the truth.

There is also demonic activity around us. These demons are ones that are not interested in us, but are dealing with something else, and we happen to get into their zone. Just as there is an "aroma of Christ" around believers and where His presence is, so there is a distasteful spiritual odor around demons. A believer trained in the gift of discernment picks up the scent like a bloodhound.

A friend of mine was being trained in the gift of discernment and learned to pay attention to his own thoughts, emotions, and reactions. If he came into a room, for example, and suddenly started to feel downhearted or confused, he could see that the emotion did not emerge from him, but from an outside source. The heaviness was the aura of a spirit at work in the room. In the same way, he could start feeling angry for no reason, and then realize that it was not from him. The spirit of confusion tends to come as a sense of vertigo or disorientation. If there were spirits of perversion roaming, he would be faced with all kinds of eye-catching women or hear his unsaved co-workers suddenly give themselves to dirty jokes or obscene talk. Leaving the workplace, things would suddenly become normal again.

When you start feeling helpless against a flood of emotions welling up at a moment's notice, when sudden feelings of anger, lust, or jealousy (to name a few) emerge, start praying! Command that spirit to leave, and pray for those around you to be set free. Renounce any participation with this spirit and confess any sin. If you still feel guilty, recognize it as a smokescreen to keep you in the dark. You are not condemned by God; you are simply under attack from your enemy.

The purpose of all evil spirits is to control you and keep you fighting against your own fellow soldiers. It is the delight of the enemy to see the disunity and jealousy that destroys our witness and separates close friends. Let us not give him any more of our time or let him drain away our lives. Let us agree with God, stand on His eternal Word, and resist the devil—he *will* flee from us! (See James 4:7.)

LORD OF THE FLIES

In the New Testament, Jesus referred to satan as "beelzebub" (see Matt. 12:27; Luke 11:18). In translation, this name means "lord of the flies." Flies are pesky little insects that come in mass. They are not dangerous in one sense and are easily killed. But as they travel around, they pick up and transfer disease. Their strength is in number and in planting infection. They feast on carnage and rot.

The Song of Songs warns us to watch out for the little things that spoil us from bearing fruit. *Catch for us the foxes, the little foxes that ruin the vineyard, our vineyards that are in bloom* (Song of Sol. 2:15).

In this section, I have received most of my understanding from experience, the experiences of my husband and our common friends, from testimonies of other believers dealing with counseling, and from the teachings of Derek Prince.

There seems to be distinct differences between fallen angels and evil spirits. Angels are naturally Heaven-bound, while evil spirits are earth-bound. Angels seem to want to control or influence a geographical area, while the very desire of an evil spirit is to occupy and control a body and make it its home. Angels are majestic beings, while many evil spirits display petty characters: they whine; they are weak and fearful; they argue; and they are quick to flee when confronted. The demon-possessed man among the tombs confessed to have a legion (well over a thousand) of evil spirits in his body before Jesus drove them out. Jesus also mentioned that an evil spirit will try to return to a man's body if he is driven out, and he may take several others with him (see Luke 11:24-26). They are like flies, feasting on their control of a human body and lusting to make it serve them.

It is *very common* for believers to be harassed and worn down by evil spirits that have found an entry of permission, mainly through unbroken curses, worldly thinking patterns, or agreement with lies. The Lord delivered me some years back from a harassing spirit that had followed me for 15 years in the form of despair. My ignorance was a shield for it to continue, but I also accepted the lies it presented and so allowed it to influence me. When it was in a mood to torment me, it played my thoughts of discouragement and hopelessness until the day was ruined. *But...*the same hour the Lord revealed to me that this was not me going crazy, but rather a spirit sent to torment me, it was conquered. Until then, every time I let my thoughts be ruled by despondency or lies, they were "my flies," swarming around and distracting my service to the Lord.

I think there are countless numbers of "flies" that are on assignment against us to bring us down, to distract us, to torment us, and to incapacitate us from bearing fruit for God. These flies are overcome by the renewal of our minds (the intake and meditation of God's Word) and taking captive all thoughts to obey Christ (see 2 Cor. 10:5). This is no small war, my friends! And painfully enough, the only thing that will shield us is the continuous and conscious discipline of steering our thought lives, rejecting all subtle introductions, and accepting the responsibility of what we feed it.

We may also encounter days of fly infestation! These are the accumulative stresses of many things "going wrong" in the same day. "When it's raining, it's pouring" goes the saying that very well describes the attack of the flies. My husband has learned to discern these kinds of attacks to wear us down. There are nights when several children have nightmares or are sick; they cannot sleep in their own beds, or they need a drink of water, or the baby wakes up and wants to play. This is not normal! We deal with all the troubles, and then we pray for protection and expel the invisible intruders. Numerous times we have experienced complete peace the rest of the night, fevers breaking, and no more bad dreams. But if we do not pray, the flies still fly around to their hearts' content. These incidents are not necessarily super-difficult circumstances, but they are irritating and tiring. Try to go to sleep in a room with only one fly buzzing around in the dark! Most of us could not rest until we turned on the light, grabbed the fly swatter, and made an end to that pest.

In many cases the swatting of flies is our first action toward taking an offensive stand in the battle against evil. They may be small and insignificant, but it is good to get rid of them! After you have learned to swat your flies with a resolute mind and faith and say, "I don't accept this any more! Leave, in Jesus' name. You have no permission to be here!" you will not feel so out of place when the bigger hurdles appear.

Satan is not lord of the flies in just a spiritual sense. There are a number of creatures that have a history in symbolizing or embodying evil. They are not as dangerous as they are good indicators of the spiritual environment. Let me share some stories with you.

A friend of mine, a young woman, who had a troubled home and came from a difficult background, returned one day to find her whole kitchen alive with bugs! They were everywhere! Her first reaction was hysteria, but after we prayed on the phone, she refused the torment and had the presence of mind to deal with them.

While living overseas, we also had incidents with cockroaches. When we tried to get to sleep they would come up onto our bed and annoy us. When we took authority of the situation and refused them entry, they stopped coming.

Another time, when my husband worked in a very dark place and lots of spiritual warfare was going on, he was driving one of the little service cars back to a garage when it stalled. However much he tried, it would not start. He was just ready to give up and push it the rest of the way when he noticed a black crow sitting on a branch nearby, seemingly laughing at him! Immediately he commanded the vehicle to work, and it started right back up!

Do you have any flies around you? Are you resigned to putting up with them, or have you hunted down a fly swatter, ready to go to war?

THE WAR FOR PLANET EARTH

Finally, I need to present to you the battleground: our own planet Earth.

From having served the Most High as the highest ranking angel, lucifer has turned to be the archenemy, the accuser, the slanderer of humankind, the roaring lion seeking an "Adam" to destroy or bring down into the slimes of sin and corruption. Of all invented stories and material for heroics, the ancient truths of the rebellion of satan and the enmity he has set up against God and humankind outdoes them all. We are living in the end chapters of a saga that will be retold in eternity—everyone having a part to play—and testimony after testimony of God's powerful acts will be retold and rejoiced over.

But for now, the battle rages. God wants you, and wants you enough that He went to extreme measures to secure you and set you in His presence. He gave you a free will so that your coming to Him would never be forced, but instead that you would realize that this is what you want and be able to offer up worship from the very core of your being.

On one side stands God, the Lord, holding out His hands to pull you out of your current darkness. On the other side stands satan, using all his resources and experience and tactics to keep you away. He has no lofty plans for you. He is just there to steal, kill, and destroy as many of us as he can, unless we pay homage and serve him (see John 10:10; 1 Pet. 5:8). Your future is of no real interest to him, as long as you will not be with Him. Do you remember that he is a trader by nature? He is into trading glory for himself, whatever the cost. He loves to steal glory from God and to attribute it to himself. Humankind was made to give glory, and to live in glory. We have much that he wants!

Since we live on Earth, the battle is on Earth. It will rage for as long as we live, and it will affect our children as much as it affected our ancestors. There is no escape. Satan will never give up, for there is nothing for him but defeat waiting. He will do his worst until he is ultimately defeated and thrown into his eternal prison in hell (see Matt. 25:41). He knows where he is going, although he tries to put up the show that the future is not settled and that he has a fair chance to come out on top. But he knows his defeat, and he knows that his time is short. Most of his tools since the cross are to throw illusion, deception, and temptations into our path.

With war raging on its soil, Earth itself is paying the price. It is amazing to me that the earth, although not having a soul, is very much alive and feels pain. It was cursed at the fall of man (see Gen. 3:17). Just as Eve would painfully deliver her children, so the earth would painfully yield its crops. Fertility would have a price to it; bearing good fruit would be hard. So it became with people's hearts as well. Our fallen state makes sinning easy, but to stay on the right course with God became hard work, painfully difficult.

What is amazing to me about this is the mercy of God. Before the Fall, all kinds of good fruit grew. After the Fall, He said that the ground would yield wild grass and thistles (see Gen. 3:18). I have done some studies on wild herbs and weeds, these unwanted plants that can be such a pain to farmers. The more we research them, the more we find them to be medicinal. Before the Fall, there was no need for remedy. After the Fall, disease, inside and out, became rampant and needed cures. God, in His infinite mercy on humankind, gave us these odious, bad-tasting plants to help heal our sicknesses. We traded beauty and wholeness for sickness and the desperate need for cures. And in the midst of the desperation, our need drives us again to our Maker. Even in our pain we find the seeds of mercy planted.

Shortly after the Fall, Cain murdered his brother Abel, and the blood of the innocent went into the ground. Earth was looking for refreshing water; instead it received into its bosom violence and death. Several times in Scripture the Lord states that blood cries out to Him from the ground (see Gen. 4:10; Num. 35:33-34). Earth, meant to rejoice and thrive before the Creator, holds the blood of the innocent like vomit in its belly. Until it can rid itself of the guilt, it is convulsing. Some 1,500 years after the Fall the world held so much wickedness, violence, and bloodshed that God decreed a flood. Noah built the ark, the few rescued ones with the animals entered, and God shut the door. The rain began. And earth, which had painfully held in its belly the bloodshed of centuries, opened up all its reservoirs and burst open "the fountains of the deep" (see Gen. 7:11). It was cleansing itself for a fresh start.

The flood changed the climates to what we know now. We live in ice and cold to melting heat—deserts, oceans, rugged mountains, too little rain, or too much. This is not how it was, and this is not what will finally be. It is a sign of the times. The New Testament declares that the Earth is groaning as in labor pains (see Rom. 8:22). It does not want to live under the curse of humanity's sin; it wants to *live*! For its pain, the Lord has promised that He will make Earth anew. There will be, after the final judgments, a new creation. There will be a new Heaven and a new earth that has no memory of the violent history of this age.

If you have imagined living all eternity in a place of fluffy clouds, ethereally fluttering through misty abodes of glory, then you will be surprised! People were meant for Earth, and in ages to come we will once again set foot on an Earth. It will be different in that it will be unpolluted and full of the goodness and glorious beauty that was there in the beginning that we never got to see. You will swim in the water and run on the hills and build new things and care for animals and have a garden. The things you love the best here—to watch sunsets or climb mountains or ride horses or create beautiful things—will not go away. It is a foretaste of the real thing.

The Word says that we should set our minds on things above (see Col. 3:2). Life here is not always that great, but later on it will be. Nature speaks of God's glory even now, in its fallen state. How much more will it speak then! Every time you look at what is now—observing the birds, going for a walk, looking out over waters—let the Holy Spirit comfort and confirm to you, *"It will be even better then."*

It will be a great "The End." And then we will find ourselves on the first page of the next volume of the saga. There is no telling how many volumes there are.

PERSONAL REFLECTION

1. Am I learning to discern the source of the circumstances around me, whether they are from the Lord, satan, the world, or my own sinful nature? Am I learning to discern my own thoughts and reactions?

2. If I would ask the Lord for one spiritual gift or help in this area, what would I ask for? (The gift of discernment, wisdom, word of knowledge, etc.) *Ask and receive!*

3. Where do I see demonic activity around me? What is my response (fear, anger, uncertainty)? What does the Lord want me to do? (This should be specific and clearly from Him, not what you think or hope He would say.)

4. Am I surrounded by flies (bothersome, small continuous disturbances that sap my strength and try to distract me from service)? What could I do to get rid of them?

ENDNOTES

1. Again, this is an inference (a possible interpretation) drawn from Daniel 8:10 and Revelation 12:4.

2. In fact, in the verse before First John 5:19, where John states that the world is in the power of the evil one, he speaks of the safety of the believer *in* the world: *"We know that anyone born of God does not continue to sin; the One who was born of God [Jesus] keeps him safe, and the evil one cannot harm him"* (1 John 5:18).

3. I have heard of a Korean pastor who traveled a lot, and as he traveled, he would time how long it took for him to enter God's presence from the start of the prayer time until breakthrough. He discovered that this would vary greatly from city to city and country to country. The stronger the prince of an area is, the more difficult it is to "ascend" in prayer and feel His presence. This is a good example of the differences in spiritual climates.

4. Lamentations 3:41-44 and Leviticus 26:18-19 speak of how our sins make our prayers "bounce" on the cloud that hides God's face from us. Until there is repentance, the skies will be heavy.

5. These evil spirits, whether affecting an individual or a people, are mentioned in the Scriptures: A familiar spirit (which is *a spirit of witchcraft*, see Lev. 20:27), *a spirit of jealousy* (see Num. 5:14), *a lying spirit* (see 1 Kings 22:22), *a perverse spirit* (see Isa. 19:14), *a spirit of deep sleep* or slumber (see Isa. 29:10; Rom. 11:8), *a spirit of heaviness* (see Isa. 61:3), *a spirit of whoredom* (which is sexual immorality, see Hos. 4:12; 5:4), *an unclean spirit* (see Zec. 13:2), *a dumb/dumb and deaf spirit* (also called *a foul spirit*, see Mark 9:17-25), *a spirit of infirmity* (which is sickness and ailment, see Luke 13:11), *a spirit of divination* (knowledge through a demonic source, see Acts 16:16), a spirit of bondage (*a spirit of slavery*, see Rom. 8:15), *a spirit of fear* (and timidity, see 2 Tim. 1:7), *a spirit of error* (see 1 John 4:6), *a spirit of antichrist* (see 1 John 4:3), and *a seducing spirit* (see 1 Tim. 4:1).

Also mentioned is *"a spirit of Egypt"* (see Isa. 19:3) and *"the spirit of the kings of the Medes"* (see Jer. 51:11), which further gives us the idea that demons can rule countries and governments.

6. Some of these accounts can be found in First Kings 18-21.

7. Say, for example, that a church needed to repent of sexual immorality for the Lord to fight a war for her sake. It would not matter how hard or long you fought; the victory would not come until the sins had been confessed and repented of. It is extremely important to prepare the ground for victory.

8. George Otis Jr., *Informed Intercession* (Ventura, CA: Renew Books, 1999).

9. Rick Joyner, *The Final Quest* (Fort Mill, SC: MorningStar Publications, 2007), 20–22.

CHAPTER FOUR

SPIRITUAL PREPAREDNESS

Before we embark on the study and training of the sword, there are some steps in maturity that need to be taken. It would probably be more exciting to go straight to the warfare part. But as in any army, no general would send out soldiers into war zones with an arsenal of weapons without first preparing their minds and drilling them for months in soldier conduct. It would be complete suicide to not be trained. Likewise would a Christian with spiritual power, but without maturity and character, be a danger more to his own people than to an enemy. Let us take the time and let the Lord build in us what He deems necessary. Then we will step out in confidence when the battle is on.

RUTHLESSLY HONEST

There is one attitude above others that helps us avoid the pitfalls that satan throws in our paths. That one attitude is honesty, coupled with humility.

*Search me, O God, and know my heart; test me and know my
anxious thoughts. See if there is any offensive way in me, and
lead me in the way everlasting* (Psalm 139:23-24).

The need for recognition and the fear of rejection can cause us to pretend that we are at a place we are not, that we know more than we do, or that the things that tempt us are not there. To conceal our true condition is in fact a deadly trap, isolating us from the grace of God and from the support and love of our friends. John the apostle described this position of pride as walking in the darkness.

*God is light; in Him there is no darkness at all. If we claim to
have fellowship with Him yet walk in darkness, we lie and do
not live by the truth. But if we walk in the light as He is in the
light, we have fellowship with one another, and the blood of
Jesus, His Son, purifies us from all sin* (1 John 1:5-7).

God does not need us to be stronger or more spiritual than we are; He simply needs us to accept where we are at and let Him take care of the situation. Our pride will instinctively tell us that we should fix our own problems, but behind that seemingly good motive is often a different motive hidden. *If we do well, we are worthy to receive praise.* Oh, to hear people say: "I don't know how you do it! You are so awesome!" How easy it is to set ourselves up for others to worship!

God does not want there to be more of us, but less, so that He can fill us with Himself and let people see Christ. He does not need us to be stronger, but weak enough to ask for His divine help. God does not *need* our talents, our skills, our education, or our money. He discards the value of our service as soon as He finds pride and the beginning of idolatry in our hearts because, in truth, we have ceased serving Him and are indeed serving ourselves. Pride acts as cancer, and realization of sin and repentance is the only thing that will extricate it from us.

Many would agree that we are not to be ruthless with other people and their sins. But when it comes to our own sin, we need to be. Self-evaluation is good, yes. Still, it is very limited since our hearts are deceitful and easily trick us even in our attempts to evaluate ourselves (see Jer. 17:9). Many times when we ponder our own dealings and actions, we simply cannot tell if they were rightly done. The only one who is qualified to judge rightly is the Lord. Be brave and ask the Lord for His judgments in your life. Though His fire would burn up most of your works and attitudes, there would still be time to start anew on a better foundation.

Here are some practical steps to take to stay spiritually pure:

1. *Agree with God.* What He calls sin is sin. Agree even if it hurts, for on the other side of confession awaits mercy (see Prov. 28:13).

2. *Deal with known sin.* When we become aware of a sin, a shortcoming, a temptation, or a weakness of ours, it is because the Holy Spirit is convicting us. We must deal with it. If we try to ignore His prompting, He will gently lead us around in a circle and bring us back to the same point again through another scenario. We have to cross that hurdle before we can move on spiritually. Let us not waste our energy on trying to avoid God's discipline.

3. *We cannot change ourselves.* We need the help of the Lord to cut through our bad habits, our patterns of sin, and our pride. But He is there to do the work if we allow Him to. He simply wants our cooperation. He saved us once from sin and hell, but He will also keep on saving us. Cast your burdens onto Jesus (see 1 Pet. 5:7).

4. *Learn to differentiate between the voice of the Holy Spirit and the voice of your accuser.* The Spirit of God is gentle and very specific in pointing out sin; the accuser will try to make us feel generally guilty. The fruit of the Spirit's correction is joy, freedom, and peace; the fruit of accepting the voice of the accuser is depression and self-hatred. Do not let him beat you up—resist him, and he will flee from you (see James 4:7).

5. *Accept correction* and the discipline of those you love and trust, including pastors (who are set by God to watch over your soul), your father and mother, and close friends whose counsel you trust. Many times God's discipline comes through people; just as His personal discipline shows His love, so we can also receive the rebukes of those we trust as a sign of genuine care (see Heb. 12:5-6). Bring what they say to the Lord and ask for His light and His help to change.

6. *Deal only with those areas in your life that God puts His spotlight on.* The Lord tends to work on only a few things at a time so that we will not lose heart and give up (see John 16:12-13). It is useless to spend time digging up and confessing sins that He is not asking for.[1] Let your healing and growth come in the season the Lord assigns. The quickest way forward is to humbly accept what He hands you and ask for His help to change.

7. *Be on your guard* against the schemes of your enemy, who hates losing ground in you. You may have a vast amount of dark areas as a newborn child of God. As they are put under His light and surrendered to His touch, the enemy may try to make up for lost ground by fortifying another area of darkness in you. There are many people who show off odd habits and one or two flagrantly sinful sides. These are godly people who have submitted almost every part of their lives to serve Christ, yet those one or two unsurrendered areas are so strong. May the fear of the Lord be on our lives and give us the grace to place ourselves continually under His light.

8. *Learn Scriptures that help you in the process of change.* If you see an area of your life that needs change, find Scripture verses that speak of the attitude you want to adopt in its place. Whenever you are tempted to fall back into old habits, the Holy Spirit can bring up the Word of God and help you stand your ground.

UNDER AUTHORITY

The next important thing for a soldier of Christ to learn is how to live under authority. God will test every one of us in this area because our attitude toward authority is so important to Him. It is the test of what is in our hearts—the obedient submission of a child of God or the rebellious disobedience that characterizes satan and his kingdom.

God has established order in His universe, and He has set up lines of authority that we need to recognize and agree with to be effective. The New Testament has a lot to say about submission to authorities, regardless of whether they are godly. Our first authority we encounter is our parents; in Deuteronomy 27:16 God pronounces a curse on anyone who dishonors his father or mother. A woman is to submit to her husband—he is put as the authority of the family (see Eph. 5:22; Col. 3:18). We are told to submit to all human governments and people in office who are above us (see Rom. 13:1-5). Leaders, pastors, elders, and directors in the Church—if you have committed yourself to a church body (which is important to do to really function as a part of the Body of Christ), then you have pledged your allegiance, and you submit to its leadership (see Heb. 13:17).

In God's Kingdom, He is the Ruler, and we are the subjects. He is not a hard master, but He will rein us in until the likeness of Christ is formed in us. The Lord promises that if we listen diligently to His voice with the intent to obey, blessings will pursue and overtake us (see Deut. 28:1-14). If we, however, pay no attention to Him and disregard His voice, curses will pursue and overtake us.[2]

We may feel that we have little choice in the matter of submission, but we are free to choose life through obedience or death through rebellion. *Freedom to choose* does not mean two equal options with two equally favorable outcomes. A mother can say to her little daughter: "Do not touch the stove, it is burning hot right now;" yet the little girl still reaches for the stove and burns herself. Was the mother mean to give a command? No, she was protecting her. The little girl had the choice to obey or disobey her mother's voice, and she chose to disobey and had to bear the consequences. It is the same for us.

Submission offers a unique, divine cloak of protection to all who practice it. A wife is divinely protected as she stays under her husband's leading, and children are protected by obeying their parents. Believers are protected by submitting to their church leaders or spiritual parents. This goes way beyond what our eyes can see; we are talking about a spiritual principle going into effect. A shield of God's protection is around those who submit to God's order.

Seeing how much power a leader has over his followers, we realize just how important it is to place ourselves under godly leadership. When we place ourselves under someone, we do give him or her spiritual authority over us. If we find ourselves under leaders who work against the Lord, we should seek to get out from under them. Some would stay under ungodly rule hoping to be change agents, but they do so having the law of spiritual authority against them. They will end up being the ones most affected.

We must stay under authority. If we are called by God to a certain church to work under a certain leader, then we must trust Him for the outcome, even if we have a hard time submitting. Leaders are human and in training just like us, and they do make mistakes. Still, they carry the greater responsibility and will answer to the Lord for how they have carried their authority.

One of my mission directors once said, "Leaders will fail you. They will disappoint you; they will make mistakes, and they will let you down. Therefore place your deepest confidence and trust in the Lord. He is the only One who will never fail you."

Even leaders must give account to someone to avoid the snares of sin and the subtlety of pride. A deacon gives account to the pastor, the pastor to the senior pastor, and the senior pastor to the board of elders or other pastors in the area. A team leader gives account to a director, who gives account to his agency or higher directors. The leaders of whole groups of churches or organizations must seek out friendships and accountability partners with men or women in similar positions or friends who are trustworthy and able to confront them if the need comes up. It is dangerous for any leader to stand alone and not take time for some form of submission. Satan targets leaders every day to bring them down and project shame onto the Body of Christ. We must protect our leaders through prayer, but they must humble themselves to accountability. It may be a hard thing to do, but it is the only way to stay standing in the intense days ahead.

DESPERATE FOR THE POWER OF GOD

It is not for you to know the times or dates the Father has set by His own authority. But you will receive power when the Holy Spirit comes on you; and you will be my witnesses in Jerusalem, and in all Judea and Samaria, and to the ends of the earth (Acts 1:7-8).

God's people are meant to experience and testify to the power of God. We are meant to see for ourselves that God exists and that He answers prayer. We are meant to be clothed with the divine power of God as a witness to the saving power of the Gospel. Until our personal world has met with the reality of His power, our hearts are not satisfied. We must meet with God.

The pursuit of God and His almighty power is what drives the Church to new levels of healing, restoration, and revelation. One touch from Him is worth more than all the efforts of people. One word from Him brings more hope, more correction, and more *life* than all the wisdom of the world. One divine healing is more exciting than hundreds of reports of medical cures. Why?

It is because *God showed up*, in His power and in His love. If there is a God and He is willing to touch my personal life (out of the billions of lives on the planet), then I am undone—my walls come down, my wounds start to heal, and my heart finds new hope. God has met me, and He did not come to judge, but to rescue me. What a testimony!

About 100 years ago the Lord awakened the Church to receive and acknowledge the Holy Spirit and the spiritual gifts. Through revivals sweeping the globe, a new level of dependency and trust in the power of God roused the Church from centuries of sleep. It was a major advance forward for the Kingdom of God, and as true faith rose up and started laying hold of the miraculous, the enemy was frantically trying to stop the advance. In the mingling of the true wheat (the authentic faith move) and the tares of the enemy—a process the Lord allowed—many were confused and repelled the authentic move of God together with the counterfeit (see Matt. 13:24-30). The tactic of the enemy worked. Revivals died down as the voice of the Spirit was quenched in the attempt to gain control over meetings and bring respectability to the move.[3]

But God was not done yet! One wave of revival faded, but the truth of the work of the Spirit had been restored to the Church, established by thousands of miraculous healings and wonders. Since then there has been continual reports from all over the world of the power of God—people raised from the dead, healing crusades with thousands touched, and nations changed in the wake of His footsteps. What an incredible time we live in!

We must seek the power of God. In the midst of this pursuit, we will face one of the most powerful temptations satan has offered mankind: to try to separate and use the power of God independently of God Himself. Let us take a closer look at this temptation.

Satan is intoxicated with thoughts of power, and he has sown the same seed in us through Adam and Eve. "Eat this fruit, so that you can know good and evil, and *become like God*" (see Gen. 3:5). Adam's fall into sin has made us, his offspring, live with a nature that lusts for selfish power, recognition, and personal *glory.*

Every time our hearts are not right before God, seeking power becomes deadly. It feeds our sinful nature and breeds rebellion against His authority. In fact, trying to control and exploit divine power is witchcraft! God is

God; He exercises the power that belongs to Him. Every other being in the universe will either submit to His power—and so become agents to enhance it—or ignore it or try to control it for their own means.

In our pursuit of the power of God we must learn to draw close to the Lord. His power is not independent of Him, but it flows from His very being. The closer we get, the more we will see His glory and be able to represent Him on earth. Men will be drawn to Him, not to us. Our focus must be to seek His face, not His hand of power. Because of our fallen nature, we must find our safety in His presence as we partake of His power.

> *I saw Satan fall like lightning from heaven. I have given you authority to trample on snakes and scorpions and to overcome all the power of the enemy; nothing will harm you.* **However, do not rejoice that the spirits submit to you, but rejoice that your names are written in heaven** (Luke 10:18-20).

God will do miracles and healings almost unheard of, and He will do them in this new era that has begun. The age of the final battle has begun; He will reveal His judgments on the earth, and He will reveal His glory to an extent never seen before. We will have a part in it; we will be eye witnesses to His power. Would you want to be a channel? Then seek *God,* not His power. Seek His heart, His desire, His will, and His presence. The more time we spend with Him, the more we submit ourselves to love and serve only Him. We will be less and less attracted to personal power and more and more desiring glory for Him. As we change and lay hold of the nature of Jesus, who always worked out of His oneness with the Father, we will finally be at a place where His divine power can flow through our human hands without corrupting our souls.

There have been many mighty men and women who have stood in the power of God and ministered greatly. There has also been confusion sown by satan in their wake to destroy the potential of the disciples who could continue the work. It is dangerous to look at a public platform and only take into account what God does there through His vessels. These men and women have paid a price for their promotion; they have shown faithfulness and perseverance, have been willing to carry their crosses, have handled great amounts of responsibility, and have set aside many comforts of a private life. If we desire to be instruments of God's power, we must be willing to carry the cross as well.

The prophet Elijah served the Lord in power; he also lived through persecution, hatred, famine, and great opposition to his message (see 1 Kings 17-19). Would you be willing to be an Elijah?

Daniel was favored by God and the king for his devotion and humble lifestyle. He was received in the palace, but he was also accused, thrown to the lions, and later burdened by the greatness of the visions the Lord sent (see Dan. 1-12). Would you be willing to be a Daniel?

Moses saw God's glory, talked with God, led God's people to freedom, and was the instrument of phenomenal miracles. He was also in his lifetime a fugitive, one who added to the burden of slavery for the people he came to free, was challenged constantly in his leadership, and spent weeks and months fasting and pleading on behalf of an unwilling, ungrateful people (see Exod. 3-14; 32; 33:12-23; Num. 12). Would you be willing to be a Moses?

Joseph became a man of royalty and of great influence. To get there, he was refined over and over through hatred, slavery, persecution, and being forgotten, slandered, and misunderstood. Loved by God and reaching a point of great power—would you be willing to be a Joseph? (See Genesis 37-50.)

A.A. Allen, a miracle worker in the 1940s, spent time seeking the Lord for a healing anointing. In response, the Lord gave him a list of things that had to be set in place in his life before this could happen. Some of the things on the list were: to walk as Jesus walked, to deny his fleshly desires with fasting, to do away with sin in his body, to discontinue all shallow discussion, to give his body wholly to God forever, and to believe all God's promises. Allen accepted the list for he was desperate for the power of God. He lived to see great miracles take place.[4] Would *you* be willing to sacrifice whatever God asked you to sacrifice for the sake of carrying His power?

There is a level of desperation for the power of God that often precedes His coming. The men and women who ignited the great revivals were ones who spent time on their knees pleading with God for a visitation, pleading to be used, and pleading for a city or a nation to be changed.[5] The Lord works in response to our prayers—so He brings us to the point where we are so desperate for His answers that we refuse all human solutions or comforts to find what is of greater worth.

How desperate are you for the Lord to move?

TALENTS AND GIFTS

The Lord has deposited in all of us talents and gifts that He intends to be of great delight to our hearts and be of great use in His Kingdom and for other people. To avoid confusion, I want to use the word *talent* to mean a natural ability or strength and the word *gift* to mean a divine or supernatural ability. We will start our study talking about natural talents.

> *Remain in Me, and I will remain in you. No branch can bear fruit by itself; it must remain in the vine. Neither can you bear fruit unless you remain in Me. I am the Vine; you are the branches. If a man remains in Me and I in him, he will bear much fruit; apart from Me you can do nothing* (John 15:4-5).

We can only produce lasting, good results through our unity with the Lord. No labor of ours—however noble the cause and the amount of energy we spend—will show lasting fruit unless it preceeds from the life-giving flow of Jesus.

When we do keep our roots in Him and let Him live through us, then we find ourselves in the flow of divine creativity. Many Christian artists and musicians can testify that "the song wrote itself" or "the melody just came out" or "I knew exactly what the painting should look like." Similarly, scientists have been led by inspiration and created things almost on the spot that have been of tremendous value for humankind.[6] It is amazing what unity with the Lord will produce!

Natural talents need to be submitted to the seasons the Lord gives. In contradiction to what the world thinks, we do *not* need to strive to reach any potential or go as far as we can with what we have. In fact, such pursuits will constantly collide with the purposes and the very nature of the Lord, who laid down His life for others and called His followers to do likewise. All our personal hobbies, desires, abilities, and ambitions must submit to the Lord or they will turn into idols and push out God's ultimate plans for our lives.

Does this mean that we should not use our talents or strive to excel? No, not at all! In fact, the very freedom and confidence in our standing before the Father releases us often to go far beyond normal capacity. Knowing that we are loved by God and that He has plans for our lives activates our energy and our dignity in service. We do not allow our talents and ambitions to be lords over our time anymore, but they become servants of the Most High God. Some things we would like to try out might have to wait. We only have this lifetime to be tested and found faithful with what truly matters to God.

The Spirit imparts *gifts* to all His children. We are all a part of His Body, the Church, and we all have some divine grace to contribute to its well-being. We might not know what that gift is yet, but it is something we must seek to see released in our lives. Let us not settle for substitutions; we need a supernatural gift to minister life to others.

Divine gifts come like unused muscles the Lord installs in us. He will not take them back, and He gives them without much of an instruction book. They are given by His Spirit, and He becomes the coach. *Our* job is to start exercising!

The gifts of the Spirit are meant to serve the body of Christ; therefore, they will show up when you are involved in the area God has called you to serve in. They do not always show up as inspiration as often as by placing ourselves in an environment where we can hear the Lord and desire to be used.

ARE YOU USING YOUR GIFTS?

Has God deposited a gift in you yet? If you are not sure, then you should ask. The Lord loves to give good gifts to His children, and these are gifts that will make you able to serve His will. Many times, we do not have because we do not ask.

Has your gift been released? Do you know what God has deposited in you, but you have not seen it manifest yet? Seek out people who are gifted in the area God has promised you to be a part of, and ask them to put their hands on you and pray for a release. You may have the opportunity to go with this person as a trainee, observing and learning; you will have a very natural opening to start stepping out under wise guidance. We need spiritual mothers and fathers who can help us get started.

Is your gift in use? We are encouraged greatly by the Scriptures to eagerly desire and then use our gifts for the common good (see 1 Cor. 12:7; 14:1; 14:12). There may be times when we find no ventilation for our gifts; however, let that be the exception and not the rule of your life! If the spiritual gifts are not welcome in your fellowship, you might want to consider going somewhere else or finding additional fellowship in a home group or ministry that does desire and practice them. God wants you to use your gift; in fact, He will hold you accountable for your handling of it (see Matt. 25:14-30). If your life finds no space for the use of your gift, then let something less important go and make room for the exercising of your gift.

Are you growing in your gift? Become good at your assignment from God—be a functioning and fruitful part of the Body of Christ! Derek Prince shared in a message how, once he knew that God had called him to teach the Body of Christ, he decided to excel in his calling through diligent study. It is easy to be in the flow of service before the Lord, but if we drop the task and take our eyes off of our calling, the devil will very quickly fill our time and make it seem impossible to get back on task again. Remember the truth: You are a new creation. You are not on earth any longer to "have a life"; you are here to do your Father's will and to fulfill your calling. Nothing else really matters. Jesus said, *"Let the dead bury their dead."* Let those who are unwilling to follow the Lord be busy about whatever—you come and follow Him (see Matt. 8:22).

Most good things that come start on a small scale. All we need to do is to water the seed with our faithfulness, and the Lord will cause it to grow. If you see little of significance happening in your life, look at your assignment from the Lord and see if you are fulfilling it. Start putting your mind to your tasks to bring forth excellence—then you will be ready to serve the King of kings! *Do you see a man skilled in his work? He will serve before kings; he will not serve before obscure men* (Prov. 22:29).

THE VOICE OF GOD

In the past God spoke to our forefathers through the prophets at many times and in various ways, but in these last days He has spoken to us by His Son, whom He appointed heir of all things, and through whom He made the universe (Hebrews 1:1-2).

When I was a child, I thought that hearing God's voice was a mystery that only happened to very special people. As I heard the Old Testament stories of Samuel, Noah, and Abraham, it seemed to confirm that this was right. God spoke to the special people whom He wanted to do something special with. I should not expect God to speak to me unless something very, very important was going to happen.

Before the time of Christ, words from the Lord did come through set-apart vessels whom He honored. But things have changed since then! They changed with the coming of the Son. From the time that He made us partakers of His life, He has resided in us, and *He speaks!* We have become part of the royal priesthood and are set-apart vessels, and we can, will, and should hear His voice. Jesus stated that those who belonged to Him would hear His voice and be able to tell that it was Him speaking (see John 10:14-16). It is therefore imperative that we quiet ourselves enough to hear His gentle voice. If not, we will not notice when He moves, when He stops, and when He starts walking again.

As in ages past, the Lord speaks in "various ways." He has many modes of communication. One pastor I know explained it through airwaves. All sound goes through the air as waves of different frequencies. Similarly, the Lord speaks on various frequencies, and we are the receivers. We usually do not hear all the different frequencies, but we can become accustomed to one or more of them. We develop a pattern for how we hear His voice, and in His kindness, He speaks to us that way. As we look at some of the ways the Lord speaks, I pray that you will start recognizing how the Lord speaks to you and that you will ask to hear Him in new ways, too.

HE SPEAKS THROUGH HIS WORD

Jesus is God's "Word," as we read in Hebrews 1:1-3. He is alive, and His words bring life. As we read the Word of God with prepared hearts to receive, Scriptures will come alive! People have described this as "it jumped out of the text," "it was impressed on my heart," "it suddenly made sense," "the text came alive," "it convicted me," or "it sparked my desire (or my faith)." This is God speaking to you—He has taken from the wealth of His Word and has fed you what you needed. Jesus is *the Bread of life."* Those who come to Him *"will never be hungry"* and those who believe in Him *"will never be thirsty"* (John 6:35). He wants to feed you Himself every day.

HE SPEAKS THROUGH HIS PEOPLE

I have received incredible comfort, blessing, and encouragement by receiving the Lord's words from other believers. Sometimes someone will come and present a word he or she believes is from the Lord. Other times it is just a timely word they do not even know speaks into my situation. The Holy Spirit confirms the word that is spoken through peace, a sense of fire, or a boost of faith to show that He is the One who spoke (see 1 Cor. 14:3).

HE SPEAKS THROUGH HIS SPIRIT

Have you ever felt your chest start burning as if there was a fire inside? This happens frequently to believers at important occasions, such as receiving the Holy Spirit, receiving a calling, or being in the midst of a work that the Holy Spirit is behind and moving forward. It is a testimony of His presence. It may not be for guidance as much as letting us share His strong emotion and joy over what is happening and letting us know that He is very involved. The Lord said that the Spirit would guide us into all truth (see John 16:13). This describes well the "inner testimony" or confirmation we sense as we face various situations. It is a wordless *knowing* without a doubt whether He agrees or not. It could be, for example, coming into a meeting with people we do not know and, while everything seems very well and godly, there is a continuous sense of dread or discomfort in our hearts. The Spirit is leading us to the truth that all is not what it seems to be and telling us to be on our guard. It could be someone giving us a word from the Lord, and although it seems very odd and not fitting the circumstances, yet we sense His approval, and so we accept it. It could be suddenly knowing that we need to pray for a specific person. It may be a knowing that we need to give something to someone without any understanding of why we should do it. We simply follow the prompting of the Spirit.

HE SPEAKS THROUGH IMPRESSIONS

This is the first level of prophetic vision, and as far as I have observed, many of the Lord's children operate on this level. All it takes is a mind that stays alert and tuned to what the Lord is doing. Many times it is released through worship, when all our focus is on the Lord and not ourselves. Impressions are deposits of the Holy Spirit in the form of pictures. The main help in discerning whether these impressions are from the Lord or from our own thinking is first by *knowing our own thought patterns.* Our thoughts are linked together like long trains of thoughts. The Lord sends an impression that breaks the train of thought and usually has nothing to do with what we were musing over. That is a good indicator. Second, an impression is not easily "moved"; we cannot reformulate it without losing our integrity or diluting the message. Third, impressions will often have odd specifics or colors that we notice. Fourth, impressions will often come with a *knowing* of what is happening in the picture or what the word means in the situation. For example, in an impression I had, I saw a man behind a desk, and I *knew* that he was "the big boss," and I *knew* that the office I was seeing was headquarters for terrorist mobilization. At other times when we deliver an impression, we find that the one to whom the Lord was speaking knows what the picture means. Fifth, it will not contradict Scripture. Sixth, we will have the inner testimony of the Spirit that confirms or makes us doubt the authenticity of the message. *Impressions are not presumptions.* They are messages that need to be screened and delivered in the proper time.

HE SPEAKS THROUGH DREAMS

The Scriptures say specifically that in the last days God's people will dream dreams (see Joel 2:28). We all dream dreams, and I would think most of us have significant ones at times. During our year in Kabul, Afghanistan, my husband and I read Jack Deere's book *Surprised by the Voice of God*, and my husband asked the Lord to send dreams.

One of the first dreams he received after praying was a dream of U.S. military troops in Afghanistan. This seemed very unlikely in the spring of 2001, with the Taliban going on their sixth year of harsh control of the country. But within six months of the dream, we were evacuated, and the Lord, in response to worldwide prayer, overthrew the government and miraculously saved the eight captured aid workers—by U.S. military.

Jeff's dreams seemed largely geared toward helping him in the spiritual assignments the Lord gave him. There seemed to be an endless row of military jets (signifying spiritual warfare), ground battles, finding enemies, using weapons, and protecting groups of people or children. There were also many dreams identifying the enemy and their mode of operations; over and over he had dreams of the enemy coming in twos—one being the authority and the other the intimidation—two snakes, two bullies, two pirates, and so forth. At that time we knew of no one who interpreted dreams, but the Lord graciously used symbols that we could make sense of.

Since then, we have been blessed with books on biblical interpretation of dreams and how to understand symbols. These helped us realize that my dreams, although very different from Jeff's, were helpful in my personal walk with the Lord. Then we noticed that our children also had significant dreams. One week, three of them had tornado dreams. Later, many of them had dreams about fire in our home. The collective sense really helped us see how the judgments of God were on our city (tornados) and that He was going to bring our family through a time of testing (fire), which was exactly what happened the whole year after these dreams.

Many non-Christians also dream significant dreams. Scores of Muslims, for example, come to the Lord after He appears to them in a dream and directs them to a believer.

Since all of us dream, this is an easy medium for the Lord to use with whoever is willing to receive them. If you remember your dream upon awakening, it is good to write it down immediately in a journal or on your computer, with the date of when you received it. Pay attention to the details that stick out to you, even if it does not make sense. Ask the Lord to show you what the dream means. If the dream was all in a normal setting, it was probably literal. If any part of the dream could not be interpreted literally, the whole dream is then interpreted symbolically.[7]

God sends dreams for many reasons. They describe where we have been, what our lives look like at the moment from His perspective, and what will or can happen in the future. Warning dreams are meant to prevent evil from happening through our vigilance and prayers. Dreams often come as pieces of a larger picture, where each dream unfolds another step or aspect of the Lord's plans for our lives. Other dreams are windows into the past, to help us remember or see inroads into our lives that the enemy has exploited. In all this, the Lord decides what and when He will share with us the things we need to know—ours is the challenge and the joy of understanding the message.

The Lord has in our days removed the veil over the subject of dreams. There are now helpful books and knowledgeable people who speak on the subject of dreams, and there is hardly a Sunday at our church without someone mentioning a dream. Just as the prophet Joel pointed out, in the last days God's people will dream dreams, and now, by the grace of God, He is helping His people unlock their meaning and receive real help in the increasing intensity of our battle against darkness. Let us take hold of all the information the Lord grants us—we are going to need it.

PERSONAL REFLECTION

1. Am I honest with God and myself about where I am at spiritually and in other areas of my life? Do I have some sin or bad habit that is blocking my fellowship with the Holy Spirit that I need His help to see change in?

2. In what areas am I the weakest or do I find myself the most tempted in?

3. Have I found someone to be accountable to? If not, who would I consider asking to become my accountability partner?

4. In what areas (if any) do I feel guilty? Is the sense of guilt from the Holy Spirit (specific and relentless) to bring me to repentance, or is it from the accuser (with a general sense of not measuring up or doing things wrong)? What is my plan for how to overcome the accusations and guilt the enemy throws at me?

5. What are my spiritual gifts? Am I exercising them?

6. What other spiritual gifts do I desire or see a great need for? This is my prayer of faith, knowing that He rewards those who seek Him.

ENDNOTES

1. Of course, all known sins in our lives do need to be confessed and repented of. There are times, though, that we are motivated by a guilty conscience and keep searching our hearts for sins that are either not there or that we are not able to truly understand and deal with. The revelation of the Holy Spirit brings us to both understanding and freedom.

2. If you want an in-depth description of what these curses entail, read Deuteronomy 28:15-68!

3. Read more about these igniting revivals in *The Power to Change the World* by Rick Joyner (Fort Mill, SC: MorningStar Publications, 2006).

4. Roberts Liardon, *God's Generals* (Tulsa, OK: Albury Publishings, 1996).

5. Rick Joyner, *The Power to Change the World: The Welsh and Azusa Street Revivals* (Fort Mill, SC: MorningStar Publications, 2006).

6. I have heard, for example, of how the sewing machine came almost like a blueprint to an inventor in a dream. He followed the idea, and now it blesses the world continually.

7. You can learn the biblical keys of interpreting dreams through *Understanding the Dreams You Dream*, by Ira Milligan (Shippensburg, PA: Treasure House, 1993).

CHAPTER FIVE

INVENTORY

Now we are going to make an inventory! I can almost guarantee that you will enjoy this rummage in the heavenly arsenal and treasure chamber that the Lord has prepared for you. You will be delighted, and satan will be fearful; he wants to keep you ignorant or inactive in your stance to these treasures. But if you want to step into your God-given destiny, you will need everything He offers you. Press on and take hold of everything He offers so that you can grow up in all aspects into the image of His Beloved Son and, just like Him, be sent to destroy the devil's work! (See First John 3:8 and John 20:21.)

YOUR NEW IDENTITY

From the very beginning, God made people in His image. But even more than a physical likeness of the invisible God, He created people to grow to *become like* Him—in character, in expression, and in experiencing divine life. Through the redemption and the giving of the Holy Spirit, the Lord is still working to this end that we will grow up into Christ and His fullness (see Eph. 1:23). We will never *be* God, but we will become like Him (see 1 John 3:2).

It is interesting that the very first temptation satan offered humankind was the fruit of the knowledge of good and evil, with the promise that we would *"become like the Most High"* (see Gen. 3:5). What God *intended* for people to have, satan now offered on different terms—trying to persuade humankind to take the easy route. We did fall; and ever since then, we have been tempted to take shortcuts to get what we have been promised. If you think of it, most sins are committed by meeting legitimate needs in illegitimate ways, being unwilling to wait for the proper time or solution.

What God is offering us is what He wanted us to have all along. We are meant to take hold of our calling and destiny. We are meant to know the power of the Holy Spirit. We are meant to not only be called saints, but also become holy in our conduct. We are meant to grow in the likeness of Christ. *But*—it is all offered to us on God's terms, not our own. It is an offer to draw close to His glory, not build a shrine to our own greatness. Our new identity is a free gift from the Lord, but it cost *Him* His life. Therefore, we approach these treasures as people who deserve nothing and yet are inexplicably loved and favored by God.

You Are a Saint

You were once a sinner, but God has clothed you in His own righteousness and made you wear the perfect, sinless robes of Christ (see 1 Cor. 1:2). There is nothing sinful, pitiful, and poor about your new you. You are forgiven and clothed in the purity of Jesus. Do not live as though you are still "just a poor sinner." It is an offensive poverty mentality and pride to not accept the Lord's garments after what He suffered. You must lift your head and accept that you are clean.

YOU ARE A SON

You may be a child, a woman, or a man. Either way, you have inherited "sonship" with your heavenly Father through the death of the Son (see Rom. 8:15-17). In Christ there is no slave or free, man or woman, young or old; there is simply a status of son. This means you are given all the rights and privileges of a favorite child! In a world full of gender confusion, I think we need to take hold of this and know that God does not favor anyone above another; we all uniquely and personally have a place in His heart, the place of one He loves to be with. We may be the most intelligent, accomplished people on this earth, but the most profound truth was still learned in infancy: our hearts need a Father, and Jesus showed us the way to His heart.

YOU ARE A PRIEST

Jesus, who intercedes in Heaven for the believers, has positioned His people to be priests on earth to intercede for the lost and for one another (see 1 Pet. 2:9; Heb. 7:23-27). Your role as a priest will become increasingly clear as you are established in worship. It is while we minister before the Lord that we are in a place to mediate for others in a manner that is pleasing to the Lord and that speeds His response.

YOU ARE HIS BELOVED

You are a son in status, yet you are, as a corporate Body of believers, a beautiful woman, the Bride of Jesus (see Isa. 62:5; Hos. 2:19-20; John 3:29; Rev. 22:17). Just as in the beginning, when Adam received his wife while asleep and she was taken from his side (see Gen. 2:20-22), so the second Adam, Jesus, had His side speared on the cross, and while "asleep" in death had a woman fashioned after His own kind—the Church. He is forever the Hero, and we will forever be His darling, His beloved, whom He looks forward to spending eternity with. Someone wrote that God must be the most emotional being in the universe; I think this is true, and that is why He created His image-bearers to feel emotions too. In this life our relationship with Him goes through waves of "in love" seasons where we desperately long to see His face, hear His voice, know His heart, understand His ways, and feel His touch. But it is the same for Him; He also longs for us—to fellowship and share secrets, to gather us in His arms, to be done with discipline, and to be able to lavish His love and His gifts on us.

The core of intimacy is *to know and to be known, to love and to be loved.* He knows us so well already, yet the Scriptures say that in the future *"...we shall know [Him] fully, even as we are known"* (1 Cor. 13:12). He wants us to know Him! Rick Joyner shared in *The Final Quest* of his visions of Heaven, how everyone there heard his thoughts, and how humbling, but also liberating, this became. When you have nothing to hide and you are fully assured that you are loved, that is the beginning of a most precious intimacy that we have only touched the fringes of so far.

There are many precious truths in the Scriptures about what and who we are in Christ, of which I have only touched the more crucial ones. If you struggle with insecurity over who you are or are stuck in generational patterns, problems, or sins, I recommend reading *Victory over the Darkness* by Neil T. Anderson.[1]

PROVISIONS

Early in human history the Lord revealed His name as Jehovah Jireh—the Lord our Provider (see Gen. 22:14; Matt. 6:25-34). He wants His people to know that He can and wants to fill our needs in every way. He *intends* to fill our needs. As the Father above all other fathers, He places the responsibility of provision on His own shoulders. As His children, we need to learn to trust that He will be there for us and to keep our minds from worry and our hands from rushing ahead to meet our own needs. Look at these Scriptures:

> *I will rain down bread from heaven for you. The people are to go out each day and gather enough for that day. In this way I*

will test them and see whether they will follow My instructions (Exodus 16:4).

I am the Lord your God, who brought you out of Egypt. Open wide your mouth and I will fill it. But My people would not listen to Me; Israel would not submit to Me. So I gave them over to their stubborn hearts to follow their own devices (Psalm 81:10-12).

So do not worry, saying, "What shall we eat?" or "What shall we drink?" or "What shall we wear?" For the pagans run after all these things, and your heavenly Father knows that you need them. But seek first His kingdom and His righteousness, and all these things will be given to you as well (Matthew 6:31-33).

It is interesting to notice how the Lord is rather adamant about us learning to receive from Him. In the passage from the Psalms, He gives the picture of a father who is spoon-feeding His little infant son, who is refusing to eat unless he is allowed to hold the spoon himself. Anyone who has watched a 9-month-old trying to self feed will know that most food lands in his lap or on his face, not in his stomach. But the intention of the Lord is quite obvious: He wants us to be well fed so that we will be strengthened and continue to grow. A malnourished child will be slow or hindered in his development.

May that not be said of us! There are those who have been trained to try to grab God's provisions before they have been given. But even Jesus, as the favorite only Son, who held His Father's favor like no one else, did not use His position to grab what He wanted. Instead, He submitted to His Father. He trusted His Father, even when His feelings told Him differently. Look at Gethsemane! Jesus did not want the cup the Father was handing Him, although He had accepted it before the world was made. His heart and mind revolted against the painful trial ahead. Yet He submitted, and in His need for fellowship on that dark night, when the disciples seemed drugged with sleep, the Father sent provision to His Son—an angel who came and strengthened Him (see Luke 22:39-46).

So we find that the Lord truly wants to meet our needs, but in the same instant He brings His provisions according to *His* plan, not ours. And this is where we often fail to see what He is giving and start providing for ourselves. Although Abraham trusted that the Lord would fulfill His promise of a son, the wait finally set in motion an alternative plan of action to see the promise accomplished. The father of faith, though patient enough to wait for years on the promise, caved in and decided to work out God's promise himself. He took Hagar the slave girl for a wife, and she bore him a son, Ishmael.

Ishmael was Abraham's son, but *he never turned into the promised son.* That which is born of the flesh (the ways of people) will always be flesh (see John 3:6). God fulfilled His promise in His own time through Isaac. The provision came, but much later than even faithful Abraham had the strength to wait.

The reason for sharing all this is to prepare you to receive God's provisions and hopefully learn early in life to not take matters into your own hands when the wait gets long. Provisions will come. God's table is full with all we could ask or imagine. Whatever our need is—*physical provision*, like money, food, clothing, and housing; *emotional provision,* like a divine word or promise, encouragement, and hope; or *spiritual provision,* like guidance, answers, vision, and understanding—He has prepared a table for us (see Ps. 23:5). He wants us to seek Him out and open our mouths to receive.

In 2005, my family was getting ready to move overseas. We had felt the Lord confirm our steps in so many ways that we moved forward in great faith, trusting that all would fall into place. We moved out of our home in the summer and put it up for sale. Our family of nine was welcomed into the home of some dear friends. We all got along splendidly, and we prayed continually for the visas to come.

They did not come. By the end of September, our airline tickets had expired, and my husband had to put them on extension to not lose the whole investment. We kept holding on. Would the Lord lead us this far in preparations without warning us if it would all fall through? We were leaning heavily on the grace of the family we were staying with. Our house did not sell. It would be relatively easy to move back into our own place, but a new set-up would mean losing the advantage of preparedness and our ability to leave quickly. What should we do?

We held our ground because we had no other word from the Lord to sustain a shift in direction. Some days we were full of faith; other days we despaired. In October, a violent earthquake shook the country of our destination. There were massive landslides and buildings came crumbling to the ground throughout the land. Within days, their government released our visas, and we were urged to arrive as soon as possible. How thankful we were that we could respond! We flew out in early November, rejoicing in the incredible provision and timing of the Lord.

I think as adults we have a hard time with the nerve-wrecking ways in which the Lord works His provisions. We have learned to be forward thinking and plan for the future. This is true not the least in the area of finances; it is wonderful with steady jobs, which give some sort of security and let us know what to anticipate in life. But the Lord does not seem to share this enthusiasm. Instead, He puts His children through the most faith-stretching times, testing us and testing us until we start putting our confidence in Him rather than in what we see or expect. Amazing stories have been told of those who were asked to walk out into seemingly thin air to find that God provided the support. How is it possible that George Muller could build an orphanage and care for hundreds of children with no steady income? He would not even make his needs for the home known, yet in the most miraculous ways the Lord provided for their needs.[2]

Why is it that we see so little of divine provisions in our lives? Many times it is because they are simply not needed. We are surrounded by comfort, not lacking any material good. As a Western people, we meet our God more in the areas of emotional and spiritual need, or when faced with serious illnesses, because that is where we finally feel our need and cry out. But in developing countries, we are not surprised to see many miracles among the believers because they have felt physical needs. God feeds us when we open our mouths. We will not open our mouths if we are full.

I am not intending to say that the bounty we experience is necessarily evil. Some of it is God's provision for us. But I also see that in many places the overindulgence and "fat of the land" has been more seductive than blessed. Divine provisions make us thankful and encourage our spiritual walk; manmade provisions tend to make us careless and presumptuous. In whatever way the Lord provides for us, we must remember to lean on Him, not on the provisions, or we become crippled in our faith. If our hearts are truly stayed on God and not the material, we will be able to face any crisis with peace, knowing that God will always care for us.

As we look for the provisions of God, they cover every area of human need. *Anything that you would ever need, the Lord has an appropriate provision for.* As you look to Him and wait for His answer, He will give it to you. Our task is to wait, to submit, and then to accept His provision when it comes.

These provisions are to be sought *and waited* for:

- A spouse

- A worthy vision

- Offspring

- A mentor (a spiritual father or mother to train you)

- Deliverance (in health, from bondages, from circumstances)

- Spiritual, physical, and emotional needs, ongoing or momentary

Some provisions have to be gathered by us, like the manna:

- The Word of God (spiritual meat)

- The personal word of God for you (the daily bread, manna)

- The counsel (advice) of the godly

- The fellowship of the saints

- The fellowship of the Holy Spirit

- Grace

Finally I want to remember what the apostle Peter wrote for our benefit:

> *His divine power has given us everything we need for life and godliness through the knowledge of Him who called us by His own glory and goodness. Through these He has given us His very great and precious promises, so that through them you may participate in the divine nature and escape the corruption in the world caused by evil desires* (2 Peter 1:3-4).

SECURITY

He will be the sure foundation for your times, a rich store of salvation and wisdom and knowledge; the fear of the Lord is the key to this treasure (Isaiah 33:6).

We live in a physical world, and what we see is often what we count on to be the truth. However, when we are born again, the Lord starts moving us to live by faith, where we learn to see with "the eyes of the heart," not our physical eyes. We start seeing the invisible realm, and this realm *is* reality as it truly is.

Our foundation for security will be completely altered in the process. From trusting what our eyes can see and our own conclusions, we learn to trust the One who is guiding us into the unknown land—like Abraham, who *"obeyed and went, even though he did not know where he was going"* (Heb. 11:8). How could he do this? It was simply because both he and Sarah considered Him faithful who had made the promise (see Heb. 11:11). This is the doorway of trust for all of us who learn to walk with God—we must trust Him even if everything points the other direction.

A sense of security is important for our well-being. Women derive much of their security from being loved and having a stable home sphere, where they feel safe and protected. Men tend to find security in their position and in knowing that they are productive and can bring necessary provisions to their families. There are other elements of security as well, such as living in a peaceful environment and land, which enable us to trust that the coming days will be stable with no looming disasters.

Our bodies are programmed to deal with stresses. When threats or danger arise, adrenalin kicks in and helps us rise to the occasion. But we are truly under greater pressure than was intended from the beginning, for *God has always been and always will be the only immovable part of our existence.* Our hearts, our souls, and our spirits are not meant to be moved with circumstances. They are meant to be safe and at peace, resting in the immovable Rock of His presence. Our home is the Lord. Our resting place is in Him. As an unborn safely rests in his mother's womb, so we are meant to rest our hearts in His abiding peace. We are hidden in Him; we are cherished, nourished, loved, and blessed. No evil can come to us.

"But evil *does* come!" you might want to scream. Yes, evil does come. But it will not touch our hearts if we had placed them in the security of the Lord's presence already. That is the root of the trouble. Until we find our home in Him again, we are vulnerable and open for deception, fear, worry, and trouble on our souls. We are infants cast on the street, naked in the cold, with no protection. It is interesting to know that many people, even into adult life, go to sleep curled up in the fetal position. We might be adults, but we will always be in need of a protector, a Father.

When my older brother went through college, his class was once asked what the word *refuge* meant to them. Of the whole group, my brother, as the sole believer, was the only one who saw the word as positive! All the others, trained by the world, felt the word spoke more of human weakness than of being safe. This mentality pervades the West; men and women must be strong and have it all together. This is not true! God does not intend for us to grow independent of Him *ever.* We were created for fellowship. As His people, He created us to function as a body (the Body of Christ), not as free-cells! We do not grow strong by independence. Indeed, that is the very lie of satan to keep us from becoming too strong for him! The Word says that when we are the Lord's, five of us will put a hundred enemies to flight, but a hundred of us will make ten thousand flee (see Lev. 26:8). That is the strength of unity that the Lord wants to give! Neither are we meant to "grow up" and become less needy of God. The life of Jesus clearly shows that He always did all things out of His oneness with the Father, never using divine power for His own reasons.

Planet Earth is all in all a very unsafe place to be in. If we had our hearts wrapped in the false security of our circumstances, we would be very foolish. The economy is rocking; the threat of terrorist attacks is real. The East continues to be a hotbed of trouble and war. Is Earth a safe place anywhere? It will be clearly seen in days to come where our hearts are truly at. Those who have not learned to live in the home of God will be melting in fear together with the nations. But there is a place, a secure place, that no person can remove us from, and that place is in God.

> *If you look at the world, you will be distressed;*
> *If you look within, you will be depressed;*
> *But if you look at Christ, you will be at rest.*
> —Corrie ten Boom[3]

WEAPONRY

Finally, be strong in the Lord and in His mighty power. Put on the full armor of God, so that you can take your stand against the devil's schemes. For our struggle is not against flesh and blood, but against the rulers, against the authorities, against the powers of this dark world, and against the spiritual forces of evil in the heavenly realms. Therefore put on the full armor of God, so that when the day of evil comes, you may be able to stand your ground, and after you have done everything, to stand.

Stand firm then, with the belt of truth buckled around your waist, with the breastplate of righteousness in place, and with your feet fitted with the readiness that comes from the gospel of peace. In addition to all this, take up the shield of faith, with which you can extinguish all the flaming arrows of the evil one. Take the helmet of salvation and the sword of the Spirit, which is the Word of God. And pray in the Spirit on all occasions with all kinds of prayers and requests. With this in mind, be alert and always keep on praying for the saints (Ephesians 6:10-18).

Spiritual battles are fought with spiritual strength.[4] Flesh cannot accomplish the purposes of God. As Isaiah 26:12 says, *"...All that we have accomplished You have done for us."* It is not we who chase demons to flight; it is the power of God they dread. If what is in us is the holy presence of God, they will flee.

We are in need of this armor because our enemy is scheming against us. If we only look at the surface and physical side of life, it might seem that all the evil that befalls us is from natural sources. But when we look behind, we often find our enemy watching to see how he can gain advantage over us through the new circumstances. He may be the instigator of our trouble, or he may simply be using it to make us fall. The point is, he is scheming, and we must be aware of him. To ignore the devil is to play into his hand.

We must identify where the battle lies. It is a battle in the unseen and cannot be won by carnal weapons. This was the great mistake of the Crusades. The Christians saw the Muslims taking Jerusalem, the holy city, and decided to fight a *holy war* and retake it. They may very well have read the Old Testament stories of war and God's favor on the Israelites to believe this was a right thing to do. What they did not realize was that they were playing into satan's trap, creating a bloodbath and such enmity between Muslims and Christians that we are still reeling from it.

We are not fighting against people, but for people. To do this, we must recognize that all humankind is in bondage to sin and the *"prince of the power of the air"* (Eph. 2:2 NASB). All who have not been born again into God's Kingdom are subject to slavery to the kingdom of darkness. We must learn to separate the individual in our minds from the evil that we fight. Paul states in Ephesians that we are fighting the evil influence that is affecting humankind—rulers, authorities, powers, and spiritual forces of evil in the heavenly realms. We are not to succumb to their influence, but rather live so as to destroy their strongholds.

Paul's concern was for the believers who would be facing "the day of evil." Those days have come. My husband and I have both had dreams of facing a world where lawlessness had been released. For us who are entering into the battle of the last days, we must be more vigilant than any other generation. We will need the full armor of God. We are going to take some time looking at the different aspects of the armor so that we can get a better grasp on their importance and practical use.

A friend of mine shared how he had been impacted by the revelation that the armor, in all its aspects, is a representation of being clothed with Christ. As we go through the pieces of the armor, we will see how true this is. Jesus is the truth; He is our righteousness and the core of the Good News; He is our salvation, our shield, and the very Word of God. While some people daily speak and act out putting on the armor of God, others meditate on and trust in the all-sufficiency of Christ. They are both expressions of the same faith: our stand against evil and our protection comes through knowing and applying the provision God has made through His Son. Being clothed in Him is being clothed in an impenetrable armor. Let us press on to understand and take hold of all that He offers!

THE BELT OF TRUTH

The connotation of wearing a belt is that of having pulled oneself together, both mentally and physically, having the loose garments tucked in so as to be ready for work or battle, with nothing hindering one's movement.

To not have our belt tightened signifies being undone, taken by surprise, or demoralized. Knowing the truth that God has revealed to us through the Scriptures and having been taught by the Holy Spirit of our identity and role in the Kingdom will act as a belt for us. It will keep us moving toward our goal, and we will not be taken off guard by distractions or other's concerns being voiced. Knowing the truth that He is holding our innermost being together will safeguard us against the lies and deceptions that others may succumb to.

THE BREASTPLATE OF RIGHTEOUSNESS

A breastplate in a war situation is one of your best defenses because it protects your heart and your life. By the provision of God, your life is shielded by the righteousness of the sinless Lamb of God. Death cannot harm you anymore. First Corinthians states that *"The sting of death is sin, and the power of sin is the law"* (1 Cor. 15:56). The requirements of the law were fulfilled by Christ. He stood righteous through every test, and on the cross His righteousness was imputed to those who accept His sacrifice.

You will know if the breastplate is in place over your heart. If you are still striving to please the Lord with works and trying to do good then you are still not trusting His righteousness, but hoping that your own will do. Isaiah 64:6 says that *"...all our righteous acts are like filthy rags...."* They will have no power to protect you from the skilled assault of the master accuser. He knows we are guilty; he knows of our sins and our weaknesses. He knows we do not measure up. In ourselves we have no standing before God. Our deliverance is in recognizing that he is right; then *every* attack of satan against us is thwarted. He is hoping to destroy us on the basis of our unworthiness, but finds himself up against the righteousness of Christ instead.

SHOES OF READINESS

Feet and shoes represent works or service. Since the days of Job, satan likes to boast that God's people serve out of wrong motives. We serve only if we will gain some material blessing or know that God will do something in return for our service. He was proved wrong with Job, and he will keep being proven wrong. God's people work in response to what God has already done. Although we look forward to future rewards, we serve God because He has proven Himself to be worthy to be served. If we do not have that revelation, no amount of threats and offers can keep our hearts steadfast in service. Peace with God—which is the message of the Gospel—is what motivates people to serve God faithfully and with a passionate heart.

Having our feet fitted with *the readiness that comes from the Gospel of peace* also means that we are moved to action by the Gospel. As we start walking, we help, teach, preach, and serve our neighbors and those around the world.

Peace is a strong defense against attacks from the enemy. Romans 16:20 says that *"the God of peace will soon crush satan under your feet...."* Peace is more powerful than might! He has nothing to stand on when faced with a saint abiding in God's peace.

When we are shod with peace, we can truly serve the Kingdom of God in His power. The quietness of a peaceful heart gives us the ability to hear the voice of the Spirit. This proves a wonderful advantage when in battle. Instead of clumsily moving along, hoping to hit targets, we become like David, who declared that God had made his feet like the "feet of a gazelle"—lightfooted and sure (see Ps. 18:33). He also says that this agility gave him another advantage: he was able to stand on the heights. He was able to keep a good perspective even in the heat of battle; he could evaluate the situation and know what God wanted him to do. That is a great gift indeed. Many enter battles at full throttle. But once they are in it, the dust and turmoil and confusion start to get at them. Our ability to hear our Lord's voice and keep a clear head can save us many wounds and help us avoid tackling unnecessary side issues rather than the true sources of trouble.

THE SHIELD OF FAITH

Unlike the breastplate, that needs to simply be put in place to do its work, a shield has to be held up by hand. This requires action on our side. The shield is our faith and confidence in the Lord, the one who will provide for us in every way. We find that the shield of faith withstands even the strongest attacks of the enemy: the flaming arrows.

What are these arrows? They are words—delusions, accusations, temptations, doubts, and deceptions—and they are physical attacks—for example, on our health, reputation, or finances. The enemy has a way of using even other believers and people we love to do his work. His arrows are arrows of fire; they burn and wound us deeply unless we learn to not receive them. The shield of faith is given to us to protect us from any weapons or words formed against us to make us discouraged or doubt the truth and love of God (see Isa. 54:17).

Trusting in God's word above what our eyes see makes us able to stand our ground. What we heard from God is true, and we are willing to stake our lives on it regardless of what everyone else says. Stand by faith; hold up your shield!

THE HELMET OF SALVATION

The helmet, like the breastplate, is meant to protect a vital part of the body—the mind. I think we all have experienced how real the attacks on our minds can be. Someone once said wisely, "As a man thinks, so is he." What we believe about ourselves and our situation will reflect in all we do and say. If we accept God's truth about ourselves, our confidence increases. But if we allow voices other than the voice of truth to speak to us, we start a downward spiral toward defeat. If we allow statements to form in our minds, such as, "I am no good," "God cannot love me," or "I am never going to be anything useful," those are the words of an enemy. It is up to us to deny him a hearing.

One of satan's greatest successes in disarming God's soldiers is by making us look at ourselves and our own inadequacies rather than trusting in God's strength. We must remember that God never chose us because of our strengths and abilities in the first place. From the very first moment of salvation, we were saved by Him and never by what we were. It was all God. We will never measure up to God's standard, and *we are not meant to*. We are meant to forever look to the Lord and His strength (see Ps. 105:4) and seek Him out as our provision in every way. He has decided to be the great Hero of all history, and our helmets carry His insignia, proving that we are His ransomed ones. They show whom we belong to and that we are in His army.

Our confidence before God, angels, demons, and people will always be the shed blood of Jesus. *I have no defense for my sins. It is as you say, I am guilty. But here is Jesus, who stands in my defense, and He is all righteous. My appeal is to His blood, spilt on my behalf to cover my sins.* What a great salvation—to have someone who speaks for me now and on that day!

THE SWORD OF THE SPIRIT

Proverbs 12:18 says that *"Reckless words pierce like a sword, but the tongue of the wise brings healing."* Our words can destroy or build up, kill or give life to the hearer. The word that must be on our tongues is the Word of God, which is the sword of the Spirit. This sword is so sharp that it pierces into the depths of a person's being and judges his thoughts and attitudes (see Heb. 4:12). This sword slays the spiritual beings opposed to God's truth, but brings healing to the repentant soul.

So then, we must learn about our sword. It is the accumulation of the deposit of God's Word that has been embedded in our hearts, the truths that we *know* are true and that we are willing to stake our lives on. It is when we take our stand in the face of an opposing voice that we engage in battle with our swords.

Jesus went through his baptism in the Jordan River and then spent 40 days and nights in the desert, preparing Himself for His work. After this time, He was suddenly confronted with a voice tempting Him to provide for Himself. Jesus, the incarnate Word, answered with the written Word of God! *It is written…* He staked His life on God's promises. He pulled up His sword to cut through the temptation, and it fell at His feet (see Matt. 4:4).

We must learn to do the same. Scripture uses two different words for the Word of God; one is *logos* (see Mark 7:13), which stands for the written Word; the other is *rhema* (see 1 Pet. 1:25), which stands for the living and spoken Word.[5] We need both! Whether we stand on God's written or His spoken Word to us, we must do all we can to anchor ourselves in His truth and learn to confront our enemy with it.

PRAY IN THE SPIRIT

Scripture urges us to *"pray on all occasions, with all kinds of prayers and requests…"* (Eph. 6:18). This is not a call to go and have a few minutes of prayer! I believe this refers to us learning to count on His continual presence.

When we go out into the city, we are on the alert for cars, pedestrians, and occasional animals (dogs, cats, squirrels, and birds). We pay attention to street names and numbers or store names. We park our vehicles with care to avoid being towed. We follow traffic rules and rules of manner as we greet, talk, purchase, sell, and plan with the people around us.

The Lord abides in us, and He always goes with us. Praying in the Spirit means we keep our hearts open to Heaven, not being so engulfed in the material that we lose our spiritual eyes. A friend of mine once sighed, "I am waiting for the time when I can minister to people as much when I am shopping as I do in church!" How differently we act when we take into account that the Lord is near on every occasion! We do not keep up a one-man dialogue where the Lord has to be the patient listener to our ideas. Instead, we listen, we ask questions, we talk, we commune, and we share the moment.

The famous monk Brother Lawrence decided to know this constant communion of Christ that he longed for. Instead of being distracted by the many chores at the abbey and his assigned work in the kitchen, he determined to spend all that time learning how to abide with Christ. He said it took him ten years, during which he struggled with his own nature, with temptations and distractions. But finally he came to a place of abiding peace where he dwelt with Christ in harmony in the midst of all his daily doings.[6] How wonderful to reach such a place! And if it took us ten years or a lifetime, it would be worth the pursuit. Someone has suggested getting started by "checking in" with the Lord every hour and then every half an hour. The continuous discipline to include the Lord in our lives can be very difficult, but it starts the process of tuning us to His presence and letting Him have access to our day. When we look to Him from time to time, we might be surprised how much more we hear from Him!

Praying in the Spirit can also mean using the gift of tongues. We have access to the all-knowing Spirit of God to help us pray in situations where our own understanding has been frustrated. The Spirit searches out our hidden needs and motives, sees the situation as it truly is, and then intercedes for us (or helps us intercede for others) according to the perfect will of God (see Rom. 8:26-27). Although we may still not understand, the important thing is that the Father does and answers the prayer.

MARVELOUS GIFTS

To become a soldier that is well-equipped for service, we need to accept the things that God puts at our disposal. We must agree with Scripture that *"every good and perfect gift is from above, coming down from the Father of heavenly lights, who does not change like shifting shadows"* (James 1:17). His gifts are good. But we also realize that our enemy is hard at work trying to sabotage these gifts, purposefully trying to keep us away from these powerful weapons. If we think about it, God's most precious gifts to humankind have all been severely attacked or distorted so that we have a hard time seeing what is truly good. Marriage, for example, and the bonds of family—wonderfully good, and a great picture of God's character—are now uprooted, distorted, and slandered. How about sex? It is God's good gift to the married couple to produce offspring and life; now we think of Hollywood and every imaginable perversity. What about children? They are good gifts—even rewards—from God, to be rejoiced in, accepted, and nurtured. But the whole mentality of the Western world has been reversed, so that children are now seen as burdens and in the way of a fulfilling life. In similar ways, our enemy has sown suspicion and fear and misuse into the beauty of divine gifts. This does not mean we avoid the gifts; we should instead recognize that they have been worthy of our adversary's attention and should be pursued all the more.

> *Now to each one the manifestation of the Spirit is given for the common good. To one there is given through the Spirit the message of **wisdom**, to another the message of **knowledge** by means of the same Spirit, to another **faith** by the same Spirit, to another **gifts of healing** by that one Spirit, to another **miraculous powers**, to another **prophecy**, to another **distinguishing between spirits**, to another speaking in **different kinds of tongues**, and to still another **the interpretation of tongues**. All these are the work of one and the same Spirit, and He gives them to each one, just as He determines* (1 Corinthians 12:7-11).

These nine distinctive gifts are the manifest power of the Spirit operating in a believer's life. None of the gifts mentioned have an earthly origin or could be mistaken for what we call talent. They all point to God in action. In the verses above it says that God gives gifts to each of His children and that they are meant to be used for the common good. It is clear that we, as His children, are meant to demonstrate to the world that Christ lives in us, undeniably working in power. These signs are always meant to accompany the preaching of the Gospel so that those who listen may know that God stands behind the message of His Son (see Mark 16:20; Acts 14:3; Heb. 2:3-4).

Let me briefly explain what the gifts could look like in practice.

WISDOM

This is the understanding of divine things, in many cases in opposition to how the world views things. Many times a person operating in this gift has a way of coming in with a perspective that helps solve a problem, ease a burden, or bring an end to discussion. It is often a word spoken at the right time, a truth that sets people free.

KNOWLEDGE

With this gift, the Lord gives specific information about a person or a situation without human interaction. It is revealed by the Holy Spirit. A believer with this gift may simply look at another person and suddenly know what he is struggling with or what sickness he has or a family member's name or an important date. This gift is especially valuable to let people know that they are known and loved by God and help break through their barriers toward healing and deliverance.

FAITH

All believers have faith, but this is an extraordinary faith in the power and love of God. This faith is what moves mountains and sees family members saved, weather patterns changed, people raised from the dead, impossible deeds (such as jumping over high walls, walking on water, or walking through walls), and large ministries established. This kind of faith believes God for great things and is confident enough to ask for them and see them come to pass.

GIFTS OF HEALING

This is divine authority to command sickness and disease of different kinds to leave an afflicted person. I want to give attention to the fact that it says "gifts" and not "gift" here. Healing comes in many different forms, and sicknesses can be of various kinds. Behind many sicknesses specific demonic strongholds are discovered, and this could be a reason why we learn to battle certain ones to greater extent. What we desire to see breakthrough in is often the door of ministry the Lord will open for us.

MIRACULOUS POWERS

Though the workings of this gift could be the same as the gift of faith, this gift is unique. To me, it seems the faith gift sees a need and then asks boldly, where the gift of miracles listens to or sees the Father work and moves in step with what He does. This gift of knowing the Father's doings can lead to extraordinary miracles taking place, such as the blind seeing, limbs regrowing, the dead being raised, and nature being altered (rain stopping, lightning redirected, rivers being healed, and so forth). God is very creative with His miracles, and He will do things no one has ever heard of so that all who see or hear will fear His name.

PROPHECY

This is the ability to see or hear heavenly things. This can be as soft as an impression or an audible voice. It can be dreams in the night or an open vision, where you sit with eyes open and see the room around you, yet have a panoramic view laid before you. The prophetic can come so gently that it is overlooked or so intensely that it immobilizes the receiver. But in all, prophetic experiences are to help God's people know God's plans and intentions—His comfort, His warning, and His instructions.

DISTINGUISHING OF SPIRITS

This gift is the ability to know and differentiate between spirits, to know what is from God and what is from the evil one. Many times this gift will tell the believer not only what kind of evil is trying to infiltrate the Church, but will also reveal what believers, leaders in the Church, and newcomers are up against or succumbing to spiritually. It is a most valuable gift to have in any church or meeting because it keeps the flock safe and leaders accountable. People with this gift are set as door guards to protect God's people and God's work and to alert leadership to trouble trying to enter.

SPEAKING IN DIFFERENT TONGUES

There is a personal form of speaking in tongues that seems to be available for those who ask for it from the Lord. The personal speaking in tongues is not the same as this gift. This gift of different tongues is for the common good among believers. The one speaking knows he has a message from God, and he delivers it. The use of this gift is linked to the knowledge that what is going to be spoken also is meant to be interpreted.

THE INTERPRETATION OF TONGUES

This gift is an essential part for the gift of different tongues to work properly. In many instances, a believer with the gift of tongues will not speak out unless the Lord also grants the interpretation, that there may not be confusion in the house of God. Yet, it seems that the Lord would prefer that the interpretation would come through another believer, so that all may know that the message is established by two or three witnesses. Tongues and interpretation are one of the ways the Lord communicates with His Church in order to bring encouragement, rebuke, a warning, or simply His love.

For all who tend to be on the cautious side and hate the thought of making mistakes—the gifts must still be exercised. God knows we are in training, and He will not make us accountable for devastating mistakes that were beyond our understanding. All things, even mistakes, will turn out for good if we did them out of love for God—that is a promise (see Rom. 8:28). If we feel God has given us a word or an understanding to help someone, let us deliver it in humility. If we state, "I *believe (I think; I feel)* the Lord wants me to share (do) this..." then we have safeguarded ourselves from being presumptuous against the Holy Spirit. It is generally better to step out and make a mistake trying to minister God's grace than to end up missing a

God-sent appointment. If we act in love toward the one He sends us to, that will shine through even if we miss the mark. In the meantime, we gather experience. It is training; see it as training. He is God, and we are learning to become His channels.

We have finished the walkthrough now. There are so many more things that could be said, but I hope that your heart is encouraged in the knowledge that the Lord has left us such great provisions to finish our tasks well. With the provisions He has left us the best gift of all—the Holy Spirit, His own presence to go with us and to teach us how to proceed forward. Let Him guide you, equip you, and send you out as one who has taken hold of His gifts, His divine protection, and His armor; as one who has found the sword and is standing ready to move out and face the future. Oh, may you not turn back—may *you* turn into one of His mighty ones! Do not settle for anything less than His highest desire for your life!

Come now. It is time to be trained in the sword.

PERSONAL REFLECTION

1. When I read about my identity in Christ, that I am a saint, a son, a priest, and His beloved, which one do I have the hardest time identifying myself with or accepting? What three Scriptures will I choose to memorize to help me accept God's truth? (You can use a Bible index to help you find verses that apply.)

2. In what areas of my life do I need God's provision right now?

3. What could I change in my lifestyle to ensure that I gather God's provisions every day?

4. Where do I feel my heart finds its security at the moment—in myself, the world system, or the Lord? (Include financial, environmental, emotional, physical, and spiritual aspects of life in your evaluation. Circle above the area of your life where you feel you trust Him the least.) What could I do practically to help me trust God more?

5. When reading about the armor, what truth encouraged me the most?

6. Of all the spiritual gifts, which ones do I desire the most?

ENDNOTES

1. Neil T. Anderson, *Victory over the Darkness* (Ventura, CA: Regal Books, 1990).

2. *The Autobiography of George Muller* (Pittsburgh, PA: Whitaker House, 1984).

3. This quote is widely attributed to Corrie Ten Boom. See, for example, http://www.goodreads.com/author/quotes/102203.Corrie_ten_Boom.

4. Some of the thoughts presented in this passage were gleaned from James Philip, *Christian Warfare and Armour* (Houston, TX: Christian Focus Publications, 1989).

5. *Logos* denotes "the expression of thought," sometimes used to describe the Scriptures as a whole, as in Mark 7:13, John 10:35, and Revelation 1:2. *Rhema*, by contrast, denotes "that which is spoken" by God. It can be speaking a Scripture as "a word" quickened by the Spirit. It is used for *the word of Christ* (see Rom. 10:18; 1 Pet. 1:25) and the Gospel (see Rom. 10:8). The distinction between *logos* and *rhema* is exemplified by *the sword of the Spirit, which is the Word of God* (see Eph. 6:17)—God giving us words to speak.

6. Brother Lawrence, *The Practice of the Presence of God* (Pittsburgh, PA: Whitaker House, 1982).

CHAPTER SIX

THE SWORD

We have now come to the core subject of this book, the study of the sword and the tambourine. We will start with the sword. It is my prayer that by the end of this chapter you will not only recognize your own sword, but also start the road of training to become an expert swordsman.

THE WORD AND THE SWORD

The Word of God is not a printed letter on a page. It is a being.

In the beginning was the Word, and the Word was with God, and the Word was God. He was with God in the beginning. Through Him all things were made; without Him nothing was made that has been made. In Him was life, and that life was the light of men. The light shines in the darkness, but the darkness has not understood it (John 1:1-5).

Jesus is the Word of God. When He created the world, He simply spoke, saying, *"Let there be..."* But that Word was embodying the fullness of the Godhead. The Scriptures are clear; the world was created through Jesus.

When God speaks, His own being is involved in action because He *is* the Word—it is Him acting in His power, His character, and His purposes. He does not send letters from a faraway place, but in His Word He draws near to touch His creation.

In Revelation 1:12-17, John describes a vision in which he saw Jesus in revealed glory. Out of His mouth came a sharp, double-edged sword. We get the instant message that whatever comes out of His mouth will come with power. There are no idle words with Him.

> *For the Word of God is living and active. Sharper than any double-edged sword, it penetrates even to dividing soul and spirit, joints and marrow; it judges the thoughts and attitudes of the heart* (Hebrews 4:12).

Looking at the earthly life of Jesus, from what He said and did, we see that He did all things in accordance with the character and will of God. He even said, *"...I do nothing on My own, but speak just what the Father has taught Me"* (John 8:28). We see how this unity with the Father in word and deed released life and miracles wherever He went.

The miracles of Jesus were astounding displays of divine power. Many of the miracles were done by Him simply speaking a word or through a simple touch. But in all the commotion, He was not moved. The demonstrations of power were just that—demonstrations. He had even greater plans for His Father's glory.

> *I tell you the truth, anyone who has faith in Me will do what I have been doing. He will do even greater things than these, because I am going to the Father. And I will do whatever you ask in My name, so that the Son may bring glory to the Father* (John 14:12-13).

I tell you the truth: It is for your good that I am going away. Unless I go away, the Counselor will not come to you; but if I go, I will send Him to you (John 16:7).

Jesus is God in bodily form. When He ascended to take His place beside the Father, He sent the Holy Spirit. Rather than walking among people, He took His dwelling in them, in those who acknowledged Him.

Pentecost must have sent the enemy camp into absolute chaos. All God's people now shared His Spirit and were given swords—and these were not any kind of swords; they were *"the sword of the Spirit, which is the Word of God"* (Eph. 6:17).

God lives in us. We are not gods, and we never will be. The Lord alone is God, but He has made us His dwelling place! We can learn to walk in oneness with Him, and when He speaks through us it is *Him* at work—the same God who created the universe and raised Jesus from the dead.

The sword of the Spirit is the Word of God—His presence living in us, allowed to do His work because of our surrender to Him. He made Adam and his offspring lords of the earth—what we decide will happen. But we are in the incredible position of having been chosen to be His home, and if we allow Him to be Lord—then watch out, world! He will continue the work He did on earth—healing, restoring, proclaiming, and raising the dead.

We have been given a sword. His name is Jesus, and He has made His home in us through the Holy Spirit. He wants us to learn to use this sword—to train ourselves to see what He is doing, hear what He is saying, and release it on earth through our agreement with Him.

Are you ready to train?

THE USE OF THE SWORD

The first question we may want to ask is: Why do we need spiritual swords? They are meant, as Ephesians 6:11-13 states, to help us take our stand against the archenemy of God and humankind: satan and his fallen angels. From the Commander of the Armies, who *is* the Word of God and who has the great sword, comes our commission to become one with His purposes to destroy all the works of the evil one (see 1 John 3:8). It will be done through His power, and so we use our swords at His initiative, led by His Spirit, and not on our own accord.

Spiritual swords are needed because the unseen fetters and bondages people wrestle with are real, and our weapons must be real to combat them. Todd Bentley, the man who first helped me understand that our calling is to see what the Father is doing and release it on earth, said in one meeting that he had seen what generational curses looked like in the spiritual realm; they were thick as a man's arm and strong as a cable, stretching from one generation to another, from grandparents to parents to children. Our swords are meant to deal with spiritual reality. Although unseen, it is no less real. Here are some things that we use a sword for:

- To cut through darkness

- To change the spiritual outcome of a situation

- To declare what we see or hear from the Lord (His desires and decrees)

- To partake in the work of the Lord

- To be trained for our destiny as children of the Holy One

- To defend that which we love, our lives, and our families

- To break through regions of darkness and free captives

- To bind the plans of satan and free the plans of God on earth

- To execute God's judgments on nations

- To intersect and hinder satanic assignments

- To break bondages, disease, and demon possession

- To answer temptations

- To combat lies and deception

As we advance to higher levels of revelation and warfare, it becomes more and more important to anchor ourselves in His Word to not lose our footing. For every advance we also advance higher on the enemy's black list—those he needs removed or immobilized because of their damage to his schemes. Driving our swords deep into the ground and using them to hold our ground becomes essential.[1] We become increasingly dependent on the truth and power of God and less prone to trust our own strength.

We anchor ourselves in His Word by diligent study. When we are not in battle, we must not be idle, but tend to our swords for the next round. We read, memorize, study, search, and pray over His Word, until He releases more understanding and wisdom.

A sword's main use is obviously for combat. At times, we find ourselves attacked by the enemy, and we are forced into action and learning how to stand against him through the Word of God. The decision we make to stand and fight or succumb to a situation will show what we are made of. Giving up is demoralizing—we *must* find a way to defeat our enemy, or he will have the better of us.

The first thing we should do when confronted is to take our stand. We find solid ground for our feet as we discern who is coming against us and what weapon he is using. Once we know what is happening, we also know how to ready ourselves with our own sword—the truth. If, for example, we have had a week of breakthrough, and then, one day we wake up in the morning with fears and a heavy heart, we recognize that we are under attack. The truth that sets us free is to know that there is an enemy trying to make us doubt the work God has done and hinder us from moving forward.

Instead of giving in to the depressing thoughts, we confront them with the truth. "I will not give in to you, enemy of God. *The Lord is my light and my salvation, whom shall I fear* (addressing fear with Psalm 27:1). I am putting on the *garment of praise instead of a spirit of despair,* for I am the Lord's (addressing heaviness of heart with Isaiah 61:3). He *has not given me a spirit of fear, but a spirit of power, of love, and of a sound mind"* (addressing the attack on the mind with 2 Tim. 1:7). And so we resolutely reject the work of the enemy and set our day to serve the Lord. In such a situation it is great to blast the home with praise, declaring the Lord and His glory until our hearts are again joyful and at peace.

There have been times in church, during a worship watch, when the atmosphere has been so heavy that no one seems able to engage. That is the enemy coming in! Simply refusing the heaviness and raising your hands, declaring the power and glory of God, can break the hold on us and sometimes over the room. My husband taught me to grip my sword and wave my arm in the air (physically) when my mind would be too dense to engage. This simple act of engagement would often be enough to release new confidence and the will to press forward.

Let us not be timid in believing that there truly is a sword in our hands. It is just as real as the truth that the Holy Spirit resides in us and is working out the will of God in our bodies. The sword is as real as the enemy we are facing. We need our swords—we need *the* sword of the Spirit, the sword that penetrates, demolishes, and scatters our enemies and brings healing and deliverance to His people.

THE AUTHORITY OF THE SWORD

If you are not yet accustomed to your sword, you may wonder how in the world you can tell when you are actually using it, compared to trying to make things happen on your own. That is a good question. Authority to use the sword comes from the Holy Spirit. It is His quickening that makes us able to use the sword and see change. This authority will be felt in these areas:

- *Following orders:* When we follow the directions of the Holy Spirit, we move in His authority.

- *Position, assignment, and calling:* When we have been assigned a mission or been called to a task, we move in our positional authority. His authority backs our service. If He has spoken over us of a position we have before Him, we are meant to execute His will in our office.

- *Faith and the rising up of the Spirit within:* There are times when the Holy Spirit is so strong on us that we are moved to act. This, of course, will lead to a divine work being done.

- *Seeing the Father and knowing His will:* Some of God's people are blessed and trained to see or know what the Father is doing; then they release on earth this work. This often happens in healing ministries; the person anointed for healing ministries sees in the Spirit the limb growing or the place of disease or injury in a person's body and speaks with authority, knowing that the Father has already ordained the healing.

- *Standing on His Word:* Knowing the will of God through the Scriptures is a powerful weapon that slices the lies and deception of the enemy and clears the air of demonic pressure. The use of Scripture is a foundation of all sword wielding as we compare the message or assignment we feel pressing with the standard of His written Word.

- *Identifying a target or attacking an enemy:* We receive authority to stand and fight our enemies by knowing their identity, their name. Although targets and enemies come in many shapes and sizes, if we find the enemy not moving, we have now a clearer picture of its magnitude and can call for backup. Knowing what we are up against often releases the confidence and faith necessary to begin the offense.

- *Recognizing the source of trouble:* Trouble comes through the hands of our enemy, but sometimes we have an inner testimony that God has set things in motion to accomplish a greater end. The greatest example of this is Jesus enduring the cross, but all throughout history God's people have faced adversity and testified to their faith. The guiding question that helps determine our course is whether the trouble opposes the work of God or carries it forward.

I want to give some real-life examples of the authority of the sword. A team of warriors were assigned to worship and pray in Afghanistan. In the beginning of the year 2000, the Lord told the team to pray for the American elections every day. They were supposed to just keep on praying for this. They did, and President Bush won the elections with a narrow margin. Because of his election, Afghanistan was freed from the Taliban regime that same year. It was the answer to the team's prayers for the Afghan people. Their obedience to pray for something seemingly disconnected to their mission turned out to be the very answer they had been seeking.

The next story is from my family's time overseas, where we worshiped and prayed daily for the Kingdom of God to break through the darkness. One morning as we gathered for our morning meeting, we knew we needed to intercede before a certain violent national holiday began. It was common that a number of terrorist acts would be carried out that day, with civilians being targeted. We did not know how to pray so we began our worship watch and waited for His leading. After some time, two different people received the same Scripture, *"If a man digs a pit, he will fall into it..."* (Prov. 26:27). And after that they heard the same word: *malfunction.* With the confidence of knowing His will, the team asked for malfunction of all bombs and weapons set to hurt people that day. The Lord then gave a picture to let us see what He was doing in response to our petitions:

> Looking into a rather bare office room there was a desk, and behind it sat an important man, "the boss." In front of the desk was a young man with a black, trimmed beard pacing nervously while getting phone calls. He was getting more and more agitated for the calls were letting him know that one plan after another of terrorist acts had been unsuccessful. The young man was in charge of planning the operations for this day, and as he saw the plans fail, he was breaking down in tears of exasperation.

The next day, the news had no reports of major terrorist acts. Unlike previous years, the festival had been carried out with little injury to the local population. This story shows how a team—or an individual—can stand in its calling and use the sword to thwart the plans of the enemy.

Just as there is authority when we stand in our God-given spiritual realm and execute His will, there can be times when we are confused over the lack of authority to move or fight. Here is a list to help troubleshoot where the problem lies or where we are erring in the use of the Sword:

- Not listening to instructions

- Outside of one's calling and realm of authority

- No inner witness of the Holy Spirit

- Not understanding the work or timing of the Father

- Not applying Scriptures correctly

- Ignorant of the activity in the unseen realm

- Combating in a time calling for humility and taking on the character of the Lamb

Rick Joyner writes in his book *The Torch and the Sword* of receiving a sword from the Lord, and with the sword, these words:

> It [the sword] will only become heavy if you try to wield it in your own strength. This is my Word of redemption. It cannot be destroyed, but will stand forever. This is from My armory. This is the weapon that will be carried by My prophets in the last days.
>
> No power on earth is stronger than My redemption. However, if you use it wrongly, it can bring great troubles to the earth. With this sword those that you bless will be blessed. If you bless a devil it will be blessed and will prosper. You must be careful not to try to redeem that which My Father did not plant, but you must go forth to redeem.[2]

We see here that what we speak—thus piercing the spiritual realm—carries great impact, and so we must learn to take this training seriously and seek to understand what the Lord wants us to do. We have come to a time when God's people must learn to fight, and to do so with skill and discernment. We need to be willing to engage in warfare and not be too timid of making mistakes. We are a Joshua generation, set apart to reclaim and settle in the Promised Land. Although there are enemies who will not give up without a fight, the Lord says to us:

> *Be strong and courageous, because you will lead these people to inherit the land I swore to their forefathers to give them...Do not be terrified; do not be discouraged, for the Lord your God will be with you wherever you go* (Joshua 1:6,9).

A HEART LIKE DAVID'S

The Lord called David *a man after His own heart* (see Acts 13:22). We are going to study this man and see what it was about him that pleased God so. We will also learn about the three functions of a believer that are clearly defined in the life of David.

King David was not sinless—in fact, there were things he did that would have most of us reject him as a public spiritual leader in our time. Yet, in the midst of public disgrace and found guilty of great sin, David clung to the Lord. He loved the Lord and continued to walk with Him. His sin made him run *to* the Lord instead of away from Him. This was the reason he remained not only a king, but a king who lived in divine favor.

The scriptural record of David's life is long and detailed. The psalms David wrote give us even more insight into this man. David was almost constantly under outward pressure, but he accepted it humbly and kept after the Lord. He was a man of worship. From the time he was anointed as a young shepherd boy, the Holy Spirit was with him, and he constantly poured out his heart before the Lord in song. The psalms he wrote show how transparent his communication with God was—he poured out his joy and sorrow, his guilt and restoration, his pain and longing, the experience of glory and his times of spiritual thirst, his exultation and his deep despair.

David learned to trust that God wanted all of him, not a good front. He was honest and childlike to the point of embarrassment, not the least to his wife Michal. He gave his heart to the Lord long before he was raised to kingship—and he never took it back when he became famous. He was always the Lord's servant, and God was his King. It did not matter to him what people did—people were flighty. In one moment they persecuted him; in another they praised him. But his God remained the same. Therefore, throughout his life, David remained a man God was pleased with. It was never a matter of David being sinless—he knew that his standing before God was because of His provision for him, not his own righteousness. It was a matter of transparency, a deep love and trust in the Lord.

In the person of David, the Lord exemplifies for us not only what He is pleased with—a fully committed heart—but also the three offices of a believer. The life of David is a remarkable record and foreshadowing of Christ, and through him we see what He is building into His people.

First, David was anointed to worship (the office of a priest). The young boy wrote songs in his solitude with the sheep, he thought of the Lord, he was joyful in the Lord, and he was filled with the Holy Spirit (see 1 Sam. 16:13,18; Ps. 23).

Second, he was anointed for war (the office of a warrior). David was not a big, burly "manly man" who loved war and gore—in fact, David was as much a dreamer and prophet as he was a fighter. Yet he learned early on to protect that which was in his care (his father's sheep) and became known as a skilled and brave warrior (see 1 Sam. 16:18; 17:34-36). It was his love for the Lord (when facing the giant) and for those in his care (first sheep, and then the people of Israel) that spurred him to fearless action (see 1 Sam. 17). Even in the midst of plans forged against him, he took time to check with his Leader how and if he should go to war (see 1 Sam. 23:2; 30:8). As he took his stand and saw the breakthroughs the Lord granted, he drew parallels between what was happening in the physical to how the Lord was training him spiritually. This is clearly seen in Psalm 18. This is a very important point for us who use David as our example for spiritual warfare. David's warfare did not spring from human origin or desire, but from the love he had for God and those entrusted to his care. Therefore, the Lord supported him strongly, as He will also do for us (see 2 Chron. 16:9).

Third, David was anointed to rule (the office of a king). After he had been tested and proven faithful, the Lord set him as king to rule. David never forgot that the Lord was the true King of Israel and that he was representing His authority. In the same way, the Lord expands our ruling authority in the spiritual realm after we have been tested and learned how to fight His battles and judge rightly, not according to what our eyes see.

These three offices of priest, warrior, and king we seem to keep and grow into throughout eternity. They might not look the same, but they will be a great part of our perfected beings. Not all will function in all offices in this age. I see them as stairsteps. The priestly function to worship is the first and crucial office we all must step into. The more we merge our hearts into the Kingdom realm, the more we prepare ourselves to recognize and engage in warfare in its season. Finally (whether appointed here on earth as leader or not), we are meant to take up and carry His authority among the nations. This is the Commission that He gave His followers (see Matt. 28:18-20). We must seek to prove ourselves faithful to be handed this level of responsibility, but it is His will and desire for us.

David is a wonderful example of the progression of a believer. The Lord first saves us and makes us glad in Him. We do not start off running with a sword, but we dwell with our Father until we are secure in our position and learn to get our needs met by Him.

Then we realize the battle that is formed against us, and we understand that He wants us to become warriors. We become spiritual teenagers in need of learning from our Father how to pull back the string on the bow and have an accurate aim. We learn how to handle a sword and respect it.

Finally, our Father deems us grown up and ready to have our own domain to rule over. Like Adam, we receive a sphere to rule over and care for so that Christ can have the pleasure of sharing everything with His Bride. The future for His people is so glorious that we cannot fathom now the depth of His love and kindness in involving us on such divine levels. We can hardly grasp His vast plans, and it seems too great to accept. Still we do, not because we are worthy, but because it gives Him joy.

SWORDSMAN'S ETIQUETTE

It gives our Father great pleasure when His people stand together to fight an enemy. There is great power released when we work in unity toward a common goal in the Lord. But because of the amount of warriors and swords coming together from all directions and with different perceptions, it will take some time to get organized for a concerted attack forward. This study is dedicated to promoting order and bringing unity and peace into a worship meeting preparing to engage in warfare.

FIND THE LEADER

There is usually an initiator of a meeting, someone who desired to meet as a group to see things accomplished. This person would be the natural leader of the meeting. Sometimes there will be a consensus of a spokesman for the meeting. Sometimes it will be a worship leader who is released to lead as he or she sees the Spirit leading. Upon entering a meeting, find who is leading and follow their lead. The goal is to strengthen the advance forward, not to accomplish personal goals.

TAKE TIME TO LISTEN TO THE LORD

It is often counterproductive in a worship meeting to be too concerned with efficiency and time. The main point of a worship meeting is to get close to the Father and to get a feel for what He is doing or wants us to do. The little boy who enters his father's workshop has a great chance to learn by simply coming and standing beside Dad for some time, watching him work and asking some questions. Any spiritual authority we have stems from us being *one* with Him, in purpose, will, and thought. The more we spend time watching and learning, the easier it is for Him to say, "Here. Take this tool and do what I do." This is the essence of using our spiritual swords—being handed authority to act from our Father and carrying it out the way He would have.

IDENTIFY THE TARGET

There is sometimes pressure in a meeting to "get going." Resist the urge to plunge into prayer. Anyone is free to come and go in God's house; whoever is not able to enter the Lord's presence has the liberty to leave and go home and rest. It is better to have a slow start and hit one target accurately than to beat the air and spend our energy without results.

BE WILLING TO CHANGE DIRECTION

Sometimes it takes a bold change to a meeting to get where we want to go. It happens frequently that a meeting cannot "lift off" and gain momentum because the skies are heavy with demonic pressure or the atmosphere of the city is very polluted. In those times, the best we can do is to worship and to do so with our swords lifted high!

At other times, people may come in and change the direction of the meeting by their prayers or assertive leadership style. At this point, pray for the leader to be able to rein in the meeting and get the group on track again. It takes courage to do this, and it's even harder to do it so tactfully that there are no divisions or wounds created at the same time.

SHARE INFORMATION

The wonderful thing about being many warriors in one place is the increase of prophetic words and impressions. Many times the Lord will give the same or similar words or direction to several people as a confirmation of what He is doing. Every matter is established by *two or three witnesses* (see Matt. 18:16).

AVOID PRESUMPTION

We naturally watch our leaders and want to imitate them. It can become a temptation to also imitate their authority without carrying it. The result is louder proclamations and fewer results. It is not our fervor that wins the victory. If that had been the case, the 400 prophets of Baal on Mount Carmel would have won against Elijah (see 1 Kings 18:25-39). It is the confidence in the calling and the authority God has given us, coupled with obedience to the instructions of the Holy Spirit, that wins the battle.

AVOID JARGON

It can be a temptation to exert verbal skills or try to bring theological clarity as we pray. It might win us admiration, but it may also cause others to not dare open their mouths and speak what the Lord is laying on their hearts. Pray simply and from the heart.

BE YOURSELF

God chose you—a uniquely made you—for the task He wanted completed. There is no need to try another person's style on. God will complete the work He has for us with a messed-up, transparent us, united with His power. When we pray there is no need to keep talking to fill up space. There is no need to sound spiritual or to live up to the perceived expectations of those around us. We simply obey the inner promptings, keep our antennas tuned, and wait for God to show up.

WAIT FOR THE LORD

There is a right time to praise and a right time to bring requests before the Lord in corporate worship meetings. But there is also a time to wait on the Lord to get direction for how to pray. This often comes in the quietness of the wake of worship or in the midst of worship. There is a pause, a waiting taking place, and this can make people uncomfortable or feel that they need to take action and fill the space. This effectively shuts off the flow and atmosphere of the meeting and hinders prophetic guidance.

One of my worship leaders once shared with a sigh, "Here we are, enjoying the presence of the Lord and just flowing with the move of the Holy Spirit, waiting for Him to speak, just worshiping Him. Then suddenly, someone starts praying for Aunt Elma's hurting feet, and it just stops the flow and the anointing of the meeting. It takes so long to get back to that same place, and sometimes we never have a chance to get there again!"

CHECK IN WITH THE LEADER

Let us share or pray in accordance with the direction set by the leader. If we sense the Spirit stirring a new theme or have something on our hearts of a different nature, it is wise to step to the side and talk with the leader and let him determine the action and the time to bring it in.

Prayer flows like water and follows a course. The leader gets in the water and paves the way. When we agree in prayer or engage with him, we follow his trail and add strength to the venture. If we would come in with a new prayer direction, we are actually setting ourselves up as a new leader. Often, we will win some followers, but the end result is two currents and split interests. Let us be careful to honor our leaders and let them lead. There are usually times in a meeting where we can bring in our prayer or insight in the right time and without causing disruptions.

SPEAK IN THE RIGHT TIME

God is not forcing us to speak as soon as He gives us something. He entrusts something to us, and it is ours to care for, as we deem best. It is good to listen to what others are praying. If we have a sense or a word on the same lines, we can jump in when we have a chance and share. Sometimes the subject changes before we have a chance to say anything. It is usually best not to go back again. Jumping prayers can be the end of anointing and the beginning of prayer competition. Wait and ask the Lord what to do. It might be something we can share personally with someone or with the leader after the meeting. Sometimes we have to let it rest and take it home with us to be written down and stored. If you are slow to speak and quick to listen, you will learn much, and the Lord will teach you what to say.

UNDER ATTACK

Using our swords effectively is to have confidence in what is happening in the unseen and to recognize and then stand in our measure of authority to deal with the situation. The easiest way to illustrate this is with an experience my family had some years back. It was one of the most unusual training sessions the Lord has taken me through.

In the summer of 2002, we lived with another family in Nebraska, preparing to return to Kabul after our evacuation following September 11, 2001. My parents had just visited us for a few weeks from Sweden, and it had turned into a time of spiritual battle to see some things released in my father's life. It had been a good but intense time where we had stood against a harassing spirit and seen some breakthrough.

A week after my parents' departure, my husband, Jeff, also left for a five-week work trip to Central Asia. It was only a few days after this that our oldest son, Josef, suddenly curled up in stomach cramps. They came out of the blue and grew stronger until he was screaming and doubled over in pain.

I had no idea what it could be, so I prayed. A sudden realization came to my mind that this could be retaliation from our weeks of ministering, hitting now when the head of our household was away. When Jeff is home, he usually picks up quickly on any spiritual infiltration, and he would have ordered this thing out in a minute. But it was only me now.

Out of love for Josef, I had to be brave and commanded the spirit of harassment to stop in Jesus' name. It did not stop. But now, faith that I was on the right track had started taking shape in my heart, and I was getting angry. Satan has no respect for children, and his methods are contemptible! With new authority, I commanded this spirit to leave. Suddenly the cramp stopped. Josef dried his tears; he was fine. We went on with our day.

A few hours later, he doubled over again. I held him and rebuked this spirit again. It would not let go so easily. I kept holding on, kept standing my ground. If faith had not told me to do so, I would have taken the boy to the emergency room and given up my prayers after the first try. After all, I had prayed, but nothing happened. But somehow I felt this stubborn spirit was testing me—and so was the Lord. I kept demanding the spirit to let go, and it finally had to yield, and Josef was once again completely fine. This time I talked with my big 4-year-old about the situation and told him how to stand his ground with me if it happened again.

It did happen again, a few hours later. This time, Josef prayed as well. "Cramps, go away in Jesus' name. I belong to Jesus. You have no permission to hurt me any more. Go away. Jesus, help me." The cramps left. I was torn between the voice of reason, saying I should seek out help, and the voice of faith, telling me to endure the fight. I was getting more and more convinced that the cramps had no medical reason whatsoever, but were of a purely spiritual nature. But as the next day was Sunday, I had a chance to get a second opinion.

Josef had been in his Sunday school class that morning. Toward the end of this time, he cramped up again. They sent for me, and I took him into the sanctuary and spoke with one of the pastors. He, too, felt that it was a spiritual attack and told me to call my husband and have him, as the head of the family, pray for us. Instead of trying to take charge of the situation, he simply prayed and handed the battle back to me.

I was able to get hold of Jeff on the other side of the globe. After he prayed for us, the attacks stopped completely for 12 full hours. Then they started again.

The attacks against Josef finally came to an end. Instead, they turned on Joy, our second born. This cramp from nowhere gripped her midsection and squeezed mercilessly. I had to pull her into the bathroom in the middle of the night to not wake the rest of the children, and she, too, was taught to stand her ground. Innocent 3-year-old, she spoke bravely out for her own deliverance and saw it come. She slept; a few hours later we battled again.

Joy was hit four times; then it left her for good and attacked John, our third born. This spirit was very methodical. It never hurt two children at once, so I figured it had to be only one spirit. When my 2-year-old had learned to stand his ground, we were going on our third day of poor sleep and regular battles.

There was no grand moment of victory at the end. When this spirit had harassed John several times, the attacks ceased for good. It never touched our baby, me, or the family we lived with. It was only allowed to touch our three older children, who got to know firsthand that God heard their prayers and that they were under the authority and protection of the Most High. According to the promise of the Lord, the outcome of those days of battle was good and left no bad memories (see Rom. 8:28). Instead, we had the joy of hearing our children's confessions of faith.

What caused this attack in the first place? We identified it as a retaliation act for standing against a long-standing hold on a family member. When did it come? It came at a time of weak defense of the home, when the main warrior and authority was away. What was my authority to confront this spirit? I was standing in the place of my husband, in his absence, as a guardian of my children. What was the strongest aid in the battle against this spirit? The inner witness of the Holy Spirit (faith), confirming the reality of the attack, gave me the strength to persevere. Praise the Lord who trains our hands for war!

WHEN THE WAR IS OVER

God does not want us to fight all the time. It is important to pick up our swords and use them when there is a battle the Lord has given us to fight. But He also calls us to rest. The amount of energy and strength we use to wage war with must be replenished. The wounds we received must be looked after and healed. The battle intensity must be replaced with emotional and physical rest. And our soul and spirit need to seek food from the Lord, the refreshment that only He can give.

We can become so accustomed to fighting and looking for enemies that we miss our chances for rest and recuperation. It says in the accounts of David that one of his mighty men fought so long that his hand froze to the sword (see 2 Sam. 23:10). A prolonged fight, where we know we have to hold on to secure the victory, can cause our sword to freeze to our hands so hard that we cannot let go without help.

Some years back, Jeff was going back to our home church for a conference after having been intensely involved in warding off attacks against our team. As he entered the church, he was so tuned to war that he picked up on the spiritual influences raging in the church and was unable to relax. After struggling with this a number of days, he suddenly realized that he was still holding up his sword, engaging in a war that was not his to fight! Once he let go of his spiritual defense, the Lord ministered refreshment to him. The Lord sends us into battle, but He also sends us away to rest when He feels we need it. It does us no good to fight His decisions!

After the disciples went out two by two, they came back to a quiet place for a time of sharing, refreshment, and feedback from their Master (see Luke 9:10; 10:17-24). Some things that we see or experience on the battlefield we cannot understand until we have come apart from it and have gotten the Lord's perspective on the situation. The disciples had, for the first time, been released to drive out demons; they were in awe and shock that the demons actually obeyed their command, and they came back with their heads full of excitement. Although the Lord shared their joy over the advance of the Kingdom, He also knew how easily people are deceived by power, and He had to come in and change their focus.

After physical labor, our physical bodies need food; after a spiritual battle, our spirits need food. It is a very simple principle, but you have an enemy who does not want you to regain strength to fight him again! It is easy to seek rest in the wrong places, leading to *less* spiritual rest and more stress! Our spirits need to be with the Lord, but we are tempted to fill our spiritual exhaustion (which affects us physically and emotionally as well) with, for example, comforting foods, extended television or movie watching, games, or by demanding service or love from others. The end result is dissatisfaction and a growing empty feeling in our being. We may not understand it, but we are starved, and nothing but being with the Lord can nourish us back to health. At times like these, when we have not yet realized our need and are trying to meet it elsewhere, we are very susceptible to temptation and can also become very demanding toward our spouse, our children, or our friends. They may try to fill our needs, but since we are not being filled, it will be easy to blame them for our state. But nothing and no one can ever take the place of Jesus, the Heavenly Manna (see John 6:32-35).

When we are resting, let it not be a rest away from our time with the Lord! This may seem odd, but Hebrews states that we must *strive to enter our rest* (see Heb. 4:10-11). This is the final effort to get to our rest; we must seek the Lord until we find our hearts at peace in Him and not let relaxation steal what our spirits need. Let us find new ways to be with Him, in new places and settings. We could buy a new worship CD or get a new Scripture version—maybe a paraphrase. It is good to take some time off from social involvement and spend time at home, doing simple maintenance or work with our hands, leaving our minds open to commune with God. We could listen to audio messages on some spiritual topic of interest to us. We drop the warfare songs from our worship times and play songs that speak of the Lord's love and care for us, allowing us to soak in His presence and be healed by His love. We renew our trust and hope, reading through all the promises and Scriptures the Lord has given us and pondering the lessons we have learned. This is a great time to journal and record what has happened and what the Lord has done.

When we are exhausted emotionally, it is easy to get disheartened. Reading through our journal from the last couple of years will remind us that the Lord is at work, that He is using us, that we are changing and growing, and that He did speak those wonderful promises to us!

The Bible says we should feed on the Lord's goodness. *"Taste and see that the Lord is good…"* (see Ps. 34:8). There is no better time to do this than when we are drained and need His rest. It is not a time to evaluate ourselves; our perception will be distorted. Discouragement in itself is a distortion of the spiritual reality. Therefore, it is futile to try to "see" our way through. We must call out for the Lord's help and set our eyes on God's goodness. It is by His good hand that we live, that we are saved, that we are still standing, and that we will remain standing until we see Him face to face (see Heb. 10:23; 1 Cor. 1:8).

Finally, let us wait for His refreshment until it comes. Let us not stop seeking it until we are healed and fully ready to step into the ranks again. He has promised to so rejuvenate our souls that we will be stronger than a youth in his prime, and our hearts will soar with joy, like an eagle soaring on the winds (see Isa. 40:31; Ps. 103:5). We just need to wait and give Him our hearts. Our tired state will not last. Our despondent sighs will cease. We will again take up the tambourine of praise and sing with all our hearts.

We carry a sword; it is the indwelling Holy Spirit who rises up within to evoke eternal change and to advance the Kingdom and the rule of the King of kings—Jesus. *Of the increase of His government and peace there will be no end* (see Isa. 9:7). We advance with Him, with His praise in our mouths and a double-edged sword in our hands—the word of His authority. We are aware of enemies around us and a world in need, but we keep our eyes fixed on Jesus, our Commander. *He* makes all things possible! He will train our hands for war!

PERSONAL REFLECTION

1. In what area do I feel more confidence or faith to pray for breakthrough (a certain type of healing, for peoples or nations, for miracles, over discouragement, for the needs of my friends etc.)? This is an indicator of the sword of authority being made ready.

2. How does the Lord speak to me so that I feel confident it is His voice? Are those words or directions clear, and do I obey them? (See Matthew 25:21.)

3. Do I need patience and discretion in how I wait or speak the impressions and words the Lord gives me? Write your request.

4. In what stage am I with the three offices: worshiper, warrior, and ruler? What is the Lord teaching me at the moment about one or all of these areas?

5. Do I tend to be too quick or too slow in speaking out what I think is from the Lord? This is my memory verse in learning discernment and patience for the situation or the courage to step out and deliver a message:

6. My strategic plan of getting refreshed spiritually after being drained: (write the suggestions or things that you think would be easy to implement and stick to when tempted to fill yourself in the physical—for example, *getting some good worship CDs ready, having some encouraging books to read,* etc.):

ENDNOTES

1. Rick Joyner, *The Final Quest* (Fort Mill, SC: MorningStar Publications, 2007), 31–32.

2. Rick Joyner, *The Torch and the Sword* (Fort Mill, SC: MorningStar Publications, 2006), 81.

CHAPTER SEVEN

THE TAMBOURINE I

For the eyes of the Lord range throughout the earth to strengthen those whose hearts are fully committed to Him... (2 Chronicles 16:9).

God dwells in a high and lofty place, yet He has set His heart on humans. What we do moves His heart—sometimes to righteous anger, but other times to rejoice. Worship has a way of ministering to the heart of God in a deeper way than most other things. His image-bearer is taking time to look upward and acknowledge Him, the Creator.

FINDING THE HEART OF WORSHIP

God is seeking our hearts. What He is looking for is us looking at Him. When we see what He is like, we will be overwhelmed with the perfect character and ways of our God, and it will form in our hearts and overflow to our lips. Anything else, all the singing, the *praise God's*, and any attempt to be spiritual are not worship. Kirk Bennett, a leader at the International House of Prayer in Kansas City, once shared:

> The Lord told me the reason He has turned toward this city. You see, He has been searching with His eyes. I asked the Lord, "What are You looking for when you do this?" and the Lord said, "Eye contact…that is what I am looking for. I am looking for someone who is looking back!"[1]

God is seeking true worshipers (see John 4:23). He does not want lip service or flattery. He wants people who worship *in spirit and in truth*. He wants us to really know Him so that we can testify about Him. It is one thing to agree with the Bible and say, "God is good." It is a very different thing to go through a time of trial and find that the Lord cared for us the whole way. After that, when we say, "God is good," it is a personal testimony that comes out of us, not theology. The longer we live and experience the Lord, the deeper the truth about Him settles in our hearts and becomes the bedrock of our faith. *The Lord—He is faithful and good. There is no one like Him. He is on the throne. He will never leave me. He works things out for the good*…and on and on goes the testimony of our faith, spilling out in worship and praise.

Worship is not self-seeking. We all come to the Lord with our burdens and our needs and our personal struggles, and we all find help. But our worship is reserved for God only. Have you wondered why the Scriptures call it *"a sacrifice of praise"*? (See Hebrews 13:15.) It is because we are giving something without asking for anything in return. It is our free will offering to the One who is worthy. Our hope is that He will meet with us, touch us, heal us, and speak to us. Many times He will, but whether He does or not, it is not our reason for worshiping Him. We stand there because we want to give *Him* something in return for what He has already done for us and because we see that He is worthy to receive our full adoration.

There is a difference between praise and worship. Praise and rejoicing many times flow from the basis of our relationship with the Lord, and they delight in both our own position with Him as well as in His presence with us. Worship has one goal only: to proclaim the worthiness and glory of God.

Worship is our deepest expression of love for the Lord. Jesus said that there is one commandment that surpasses all others and is the fulfillment of the law of God—to love the Lord with our whole being—heart, soul, mind, and strength (see Mark 12:30). We do it with our obedience, and we do it with our worship. Have we come to the point of unashamedly confessing our love for the Lord? Do we have a lover's heart that makes us want to stare at Him and just tell Him, "You are wonderful. You are perfect. I love You. You have captured my heart..."?

He will not reveal Himself to just any passerby who glances His way. He reveals Himself to us when we *look back* at Him.

ENTERING A HOLY PLACE

But you have come to Mount Zion, to the heavenly Jerusalem, the city of the living God. You have come to thousands upon thousands of angels in joyful assembly, to the church of the first-born, whose names are written in heaven. You have come to God, the judge of all men, to the spirits of righteous men made perfect, to Jesus the mediator of a new covenant, and to the sprinkled blood that speaks a better word than the blood of Abel....

Therefore, since we are receiving a kingdom that cannot be shaken, let us be thankful, and so worship God acceptably with reverence and awe, for our "God is a consuming fire" (Hebrews 12:22-24; 28-29).

It is no small thing to worship the living God. It is an invitation to step closer—and the closer we step, the more we are confronted with His holiness.

In the Old Testament God gave very specific directions to both Moses and David regarding how to build His dwelling place (see Exod. 25-30; 1 Chron. 28). There would be a big courtyard, where the multitudes could worship. There would also be a *holy of holies*, a place where only one appointed priest could go to represent the people. The people had to cleanse themselves even to step into the courtyard, but the priest who was to serve in the holy of holies had to be thoroughly prepared and purified before entering (see Lev. 16).

The Levite tribe was set apart in Israel to carry the priesthood. The whole people of Israel were God's own people, but Levi and his descendants were asked to serve as priests; theirs was the honor and privilege of ministering in the temple, of burning sacrifices before Him, of arranging music and singing for His glory, and of keeping the lamp in the temple burning continually (see Num. 18).

The Lord has called us who have been made righteous by the Lamb to become what Levi represented: we are the royal priesthood, with Jesus Himself the eternal High Priest (see 1 Pet. 2:9; Heb. 5:10). We have been taken out of our nations and families and have been called to ascend to meet with the Lord. What an awesome privilege—and what a fearsome responsibility!

We have become the attention of the heavenlies. When we step forward to worship or stand before the Lord, it is not just the all-seeing God who quietly sees and understands what we are doing. Oh, no, when we start to worship, we suddenly step up on a platform in Heaven and are ushered in to stand before His throne—literally! We may still only see our physical surroundings—a couch, a chair, and a table—but we have spiritually entered the Holy of Holies, the place where God sits enthroned, receiving glory.

And we have a very large audience—right now, in this life! It says in the passage, *"You have come...."* We are already placed on Mount Zion (the strong foundation of our salvation), and we are standing before God. With Him are *thousands upon thousands* of angels who are continually watching in awe as the earth-bound children of God break through into the heavens and are allowed audience with their King. We might be in awe of angels, the servants of God, but they are equally fascinated with us, especially when they see a fallen image-bearer saved and restored and clothed in the purity of Jesus. It is worth noting that as they watch the unfolding drama on earth, they are cheering, praising God, and rejoicing at the advances we make, and they are watching with awe the increase of His rule. They are *joyfully assembled.*

And that is not all—read on. Yes, there they are! The saints of the past! Some of them we recognize—the famous heroes of faith from the Bible *and* from recent history, missionaries whose lives inspired us, and finally, people and family members who died and entered their true home. They are there, and obviously they are watching us and rejoicing as they see us change and take hold of our inheritance. The Scriptures are plain: *"You have come to God, the Judge of all men, to the spirits of righteous men made perfect, to Jesus the Mediator of a new covenant, and to the sprinkled blood...."* We are being watched by people who know us, by angels, by Father God, by the Lord Jesus, and with Him the "sprinkled blood" that allowed us to enter in the first place this most wonderful and awesome sphere.

It can come as a shock to realize that we are being watched, but it certainly boosts our worship! If such a multitude is watching us, will we not proclaim the glory of God with renewed focus and engagement?

> *Therefore, since we are surrounded by such a great cloud of witnesses, let us throw off everything that hinders and the sin that so easily entangles, and let us run with perseverance the race marked out for us* (Hebrews 12:1).

We can mold our minds to accept the truth of the spiritual reality! We can *imagine* what we cannot see, but what we know is there. We can picture the Lord on His throne and place ourselves before Him. The more we act out what we believe, the more we will start perceiving this invisible Heaven.

It is not a mind-game; it is a way of placing our sluggish body, mind, and soul where our spirit already is and let them catch up! We come by faith; we worship the Lord *in spirit and in truth,* placing ourselves before Him and doing what it takes to remain there. As we push through our emotions and push aside distractions or fatigue, the Lord sees our effort and fulfills His promise: *Draw near to Me, and I will draw near to you* (see James 4:8).

SOMEBODY IS WATCHING

One morning, when we were still overseas and preparing for our daily worship watch, the Lord unveiled my eyes to see what was happening in Heaven. The Lord and the angels were watching us getting ready to worship. The Lord was radiating joy in anticipation of our praises and was paying us rapt attention. The angels too seemed excited and watched us curiously, while they and the Lord were talking with each other. I was surprised; I had not really thought that He would be waiting for us and already preparing Himself to receive our offerings.

We may think that our little preparations, our coming to Him, and our praise are nothing spectacular. The truth is that it has a profound effect on the recipient. The Lord pays attention, and He delights in our worship. He receives it, it touches His heart, and it makes Him want to act! Think of a father whose child comes and touches his arm. The child looks him in the eyes and says: "I love you. You are the best Daddy ever." No demands, no petitions, and no needs presented—just his love. It is a rare and precious moment, and it melts the father's heart. If we have ever been in love we might remember the sensation we had when we were first noticed by our love—it made us feel like we wanted to *do* something—like, climb a mountain, show off our strength, cook a nice dinner, or buy a surprise gift. The Lord Almighty is the very essence of *father,* and the Lord Jesus is the very essence of *husband.* He loves us and to hear us declare our love for Him—it moves Him to action.

Two years after I had this experience of being watched by Heaven, the Lord sent me another picture in a worship watch: The Lord Jesus had been drinking from a brook. He had lifted his head, and His hair was jet black with water drops all over it. He was looking intently to His left. As I saw this, I felt that the brook represented our worship, and that it was refreshing Him. When it lay like dew on His head, He became resolved to act.[2] Again, the Lord confirmed to me that our worship spurs Him to action.

OH, GLORY! (I CAN'T HELP DANCING...)

Expressions of worship can be as varied as there are people in the room. It is good to remember that the physical tries to express what we are experiencing in the spiritual and is not the giving itself. The true offering is our hearts.

We present ourselves in our mortal bodies in the way that best expresses where we are at with Him. It really does not matter what we are used to or what our tradition is; what matters is that the Lord is honored and glorified in our worship. For that reason, we often have to ignore all forms and humble ourselves to do what we have maybe no experience in doing.

The Holy Spirit will often guide us or give us a strong desire to do something for God. When we feel His majesty and holiness, we might feel compelled to bow down or lay flat on the floor. Sometimes when the weight of His glory falls we will not be able to stand! When the Spirit fills us with joy it is right and good to express it before Him—we get louder in our singing and stronger in our clapping, and sometimes we start shouting and laughing and dancing! This is not improper in His house—in fact, we are asked to *make a joyful noise unto the Lord* (see Ps. 66:1 NKJV). Being godly is not the same as being stiff and unresponsive. The humble and the childlike are spontaneous because they do not care what others think. Spontaneity flows from the liberated heart that has learned to live being loved by the Father.

We are not servants first and foremost; we are His children. We are His sons and daughters, and He is *Abba*—our Papa. Our standing before Him, this awesome King of the universe, is unique. Angels would not dream of entering His presence with such confidence, but we can. With great respect for His majesty, of course, we are allowed into His chambers at any time, and He hears our requests and delights in our company. Jesus said that we must enter the Kingdom childlike (see Matt. 18:1-3). It takes a child to accept the simplicity and centrality of the death and resurrection of Jesus. It is the same with worship. We enter on the simple childlike faith that God is there, He saved us, He loves us, and He wants to be with us.

My husband and I have had to train our children to quiet down and pay attention in the daily Bible reading. But when worship comes, we let them run and dance as long as they do it without banging into each other! At times they have tambourines; other times they drum on whatever they can get their hands on. Sometimes they clap their hands, but most of the time they just run in circles! They do not think too much or ponder deep truths; they just run and dance in their freedom and enjoy being funny.

When it comes to worship, the Lord seems to love variety and spontaneity. That may be one of the reasons there are so many cultures and people groups in the world! The Scriptures admonish us to do a great variety of actions as we praise the Lord. Have you tried them all? Would you dare to—even if no one but Heaven was watching?

Sing! There is no need to worry about our voices, how good or bad we sound. God could not be more pleased than when we sing for Him (see Ps. 100:2; Eph. 5:19). He created our vocal cords to release our praise.

Shout and make noise! We may be of a gentle type, but it is good to shake ourselves out of normalcy and declare to Heaven and hell who is the rightful owner of this planet (see Ps. 47:1; 98:4; 100:1). Love the Lord your God with all your strength!

Proclaim and declare! Psalm 96:2-3 says, *"Sing to the Lord; praise His name....Declare His glory among the nations, His marvelous deeds among all peoples."* We search His Word and find the Scripture that describes how awesome the Lord is. It fortifies our hearts with faith, and it makes the lies and imaginations around us crumble. You shall know the truth, and the truth shall set you free (see John 8:32)!

Raise your hands! Fear of people can keep our hands to our sides, as heavy as lead. Our flesh will not want to surrender leadership to Jesus. Lifting our hands is sometimes the act that frees our hearts to worship and forgetting what others might think. Some raise their hands to surrender their will to the Lord; others raise them in praise, to lift up Jesus (see 2 Chron. 6:12; 1 Tim. 2:8). Some have their hands raised in fists as they stand and worship as warriors with their swords raised high. *The King reigns!*

Kneel! It will do us a lot of good to humble ourselves to kneel (see Ps. 95:6). We are saying, *"I am not in charge; You are. I am needy; You have the answers. I am the saved one; I owe You my allegiance."* When we get lower, we make room for God's answers. When we hide our faces and let the people around know that we are not available, the pressure of performance lifts— we have drawn near to God to seek Him only. *"Draw near to God, and He will draw near to you..."* (James 4:8 NASB). *"Humble yourselves, therefore, under the mighty hand of God, that He may lift you up in due time"* (1 Pet. 5:6).

Prostrate yourself! This simply means to lay flat, face in the dust (see Josh. 5:14; Rev. 1:17). We cannot get any lower. In the presence of a holy God, when the weight of His glory fills the room, there is sometimes no other appropriate response.

Clap your hands! Clapping our hands means we are engaging and willing to give of ourselves, of our strength and our attention (see 2 Kings 11:12; Ps. 47:1). Many young children start their journey of happy expression by clapping their hands to music. Their next step is swaying with the rhythm. Finally they dance.

Dance! If we are "not that kind of person," let us not feel pressured into dancing to conform to others, to no great effect besides embarrassment to ourselves. The Lord accepts the worship of our hearts. But—if our hearts say, "I want to dance! He has filled me with such joy, and I am bursting to move!"—then dance (see Ps. 30:11; 149:3; 150:4; Eccles. 3:4)! Do not worry, it looks just as silly to confine our motions to suppressed wiggles as it does to take the leap and give ourselves to jumping or twirling.

Ladies and gentlemen, a word of caution: this dance is before a holy God who clothed us with modesty and would rather we sat in our chairs with our arms crossed than cause our brother or sister to stumble. Women, go to worship in loose-fitting clothes and supportive inner garments (you get the idea!) so that the attention goes to the One to whom it belongs. Men, likewise, watch your hearts, that you are not performing for someone other than Him.

Dancing is not a mark of spirituality—it is simply an expression of great gladness. This is one of those areas of liberty where we have to see that things are done orderly and beautifully. The Lord loves dancing, which is so closely linked with rejoicing. He Himself dances for joy at times! Let us not avoid the expression of dancing—more than many other things, it keeps us humble and childlike before Him and our fellow believers and releases freedom and joy in our relationship with our Father.

Boast! We will look at this later on in this chapter. Get ready to learn a new, exciting way to worship!

Rejoice! This may be redundant, since dancing and singing and declaring are often the active steps of rejoicing. But the Scriptures are so emphatic that we shall enter His presence with joy and gladness (see Ps. 100; Phil. 3:1; 4:4; 1 Thess. 5:16). The cheerful heart has a continual feast (see Prov. 15:15). When we are filled with the joy of the Holy Spirit, we will want to laugh, cry, jump, clap our hands, or sing—we will have too few ways of expressing our joy before the Lord. It is not for nothing that the Bible calls it the oil of gladness (see Ps. 45:7). In revivals the anointing of joy has sometimes been so strong that people have laughed for hours while the Lord has healed them from their brokenness.

Take off your shoes! If we become aware of the Lord's presence while we worship and we want to acknowledge His holiness, we can take off our shoes (see Exod. 3:4). Shoes represent the dust and wear of living, as well as the spiritual dust that settles on us (see Matt. 10:14; John 13:10). We will want to remove anything impure from our beings. The Lord says, "Be holy because I Am holy" (see 1 Pet. 1:16).

Cover your head (for women)! First Corinthians 11:2-16 speaks of women covering their heads in the congregational setting. This is not an outdated request from the early church, but rather, deals with spiritual order in worship. Angels carefully observe the worship of God's people, and they pay attention to women covering their hair. Why is this? We read in the same passage that *"A man...is the image and glory of God; but the woman is the glory of man"* (1 Cor. 11:7). In the time of worship, women can cover their heads to veil the honor of humanity to point to and proclaim the surpassing glory and honor of the Lord. Covering one's head as a woman is an act of humility and a display of casting aside our own, earthly glory or beauty to focus all praise on the one who is worthy in every way. In the future, all believers will receive crowns of honor for our service and our perseverance. But we will realize how unworthy we are and hand them right back to Jesus. Our glory fades in comparison to His. The head covering can be a way for women to show their adoration of Jesus.

Praise Him with instruments! There is a great variety of instruments mentioned in the Bible, and probably a good representation of the musical tools available in those days (see Ps. 150:3-5). The main point is that musical instruments are welcome to the Lord in our expressions of worship. If we like drums, we may play drums. If we like piano, we may play our hearts out! Is someone skilled with the violin? Why not put it to use in our worship watches? The Lord enjoys trumpet blasts; He has decided to come back to the sound of one. Put some homemade rattles and shakers in the hands of children, and they will know how to make noise! Instruments are great mediums to usher in the presence of the Lord and dispel all gloomy thoughts. Play softly; play loudly; play to the glory and majesty of the King. Fill the skies and the airwaves with worship. Demons will be shaken out of their hiding places and strongholds when they hear the drums, the trumpets, and the shouts of the army of the Lord.

Raise a banner! When we are in the army, our troops will have a flag or a banner to show its allegiance to a kingdom and to proclaim its advance. We are in a Kingdom; we are in an army, and we are advancing (see Ps. 20:5; 60:4; Song of Sol. 2:4; 6:4; Isa. 13:2-3)!

Make some banners. Place on them the names of our King. I have seen banners so large that they needed two adults to hold them up, and I have seen really small flags for children to wave. In a worship service where banners are waved throughout the room, trumpet blasts are sounding, and hundreds of voices are singing His praises, it seems like a foretaste of Heaven—as if we are finally learning to recognize His majesty! The Lord is the Commander of the armies!

Dress for the purpose of worship! In the Old Testament times, the Levites served in the temple of God dressed for service. They wore white clothes and had specific belts or plates on their chests; some wore some kind of bandannas (see Lev. 8:13). The temple and the people who worked there were designed to show with the colors of their garments or materials different aspects of God's character and His plan of salvation. Scarlet stands for the atoning blood of the Lamb of God; dark blue is the color of Heaven and His Kingdom; white stands for purity and holiness; purple stands for His divine royalty.

Revelation speaks of how the saints gather around the throne to worship, wearing radiant white garments that show the purity of the heavenly Bride. All this we can use for presenting the truths of God in our worship.[3] When King David came home from battle, the maidens came out with tambourines and danced and sang his praises (see 1 Sam. 18:6). In the same way, it is fitting for us to dress for the purpose of meeting the Lord of the armies, especially in celebration of His victories!

Be still before Him! We can worship in silence, not a word coming from our lips (see Eccles. 3:7). We can stand before Him and gaze on His loveliness. Be still and know that He is God (see Ps. 46:10). All is under His control. There will be times when we are too overwhelmed by His love, His sacrifice on the cross, His faithfulness in meeting our needs, and His promises for us and our families that words will fail. All we can do is to stand silent in His presence. The Lord is in His holy temple; let all the earth be silent before Him (see Hab. 2:20).

A POWERFUL BOAST

When the Lord first told me to write this book, one of the first things He directed me to do was to study the word *boasting*. There is a forgotten weapon and glory here that must be recaptured for this age. We must learn to boast, and learn how to do it well.

Let us start with this psalm:

> *You are my King and my God, who decrees victories for Jacob. Through You we push back our enemies; through Your name we trample our foes. I do not trust in my bow, my sword does not bring me victory; but You give us victory over our enemies, You put our adversaries to shame. In God we make our boast all day long, and we will praise Your name forever* (Psalm 44:4-8).

In essence, boasting is *good*. It is proclaiming good, worthy, excellent attributes in the hearing of others in order to spur on a reaction in the hearers. If we study the word *boast* in Scripture, we find that in many places it is synonymous with the phrase *to glory in* (see Rom. 15:17-19; Phil. 3:3). To boast is to ascribe glory and to raise someone's worthiness in others' understanding. *God wants boasting to take place—it is intended to bring forth His divine and glorious attributes and result in praise.*

It has to do with glory—and that is what makes boasting so powerful and gets the Lord's attention every time. *"I am the Lord; that is My Name! I will not give My glory to another or My praise to idols"* (Isa. 42:8).

It has become the ultimate ambition of satan to steal God's glory and turn it toward himself, reaching for the ultimate dream of being more worshiped and lifted up than the Creator. He covets glory (see Isa. 14:12-14), and since he cannot twist the Lord's hand to give up the eternal throne of majesty, he turns to the gullible stewards of the earth. He steals the praise from our lips and corrupts our thinking until we feel fine boasting about the most ridiculous things (the biggest lawn, the coolest jeans, the best grade, and so forth), but forget how to boast in the Lord. The Lord's throne stands as firm as ever, but we here on earth suffer in our ignorance and deception. Like lucifer, we have turned to look at ourselves and what we have been given more than we gaze at the Giver, and we start praising what is not worthy of praise. Then, when we come to worship the Lord, our hearts have become so dull that we cannot see His glory anymore. We have traded our gold for plastic. We have forgotten our stewardship and our honor (see Ps. 149).

Isaiah 10:12-19 records the arrogant boasts of the king of Assyria, and we notice as we read that the Lord listened intently to his claims. The king boasted of his strength and wisdom and claimed that he himself had removed the boundaries of nations. But his strength had come from the Creator, his wisdom had been assigned as his portion by the Lord, and the boundary lines of any nation are directly under God's Almighty supervision (see Acts 17:26; Deut. 32:8; Prov. 23:10). All the king's boasts were indeed an attempt to rob God of His glory and attribute it to himself. He was, therefore, brought low.

Although the Body of Christ has been robbed in the past of our inheritance in worship, the Lord has now turned the page of history and has begun to restore our understanding of how to glory in our God. It has raised our generation to heights in worship that has not been displayed for more than 1,500 years. And much of it has to do with learning how to make our boast in the Lord!

In many Scripture passages, the word *boast* means to "rejoice" or "exult in" (see Rom. 5:2; Isa. 61:6-7). This is very significant, for it helps us realize that to boast in the Lord is a very positive thing. As with many other things in life, boasting is in essence good, but it was distorted and used for evil by the archenemy. When we restore boasting to its place of glorifying our God, grace and power will again flow in our gatherings. The more we speak of what He is like and the more we meditate on it, the more we will rejoice. There is no end to His glory. He is infinite, and what He is and does is beyond description. There comes a point in the worship watch—when God's glory is proclaimed and we rejoice in Him—when He sweeps us into His glory and we lose ourselves to the pure joy of being with Him; we find the river that flows from the throne of God with life-giving water (see Rev. 22:1;

Ps. 46:4-5). Once we step into that river, revival is no longer a word, but an *experience*. One of the common phenomena of a revival is uncontainable and glorious laughter as someone is healed, refreshed, and dunked in the river of life, the very essence of the Holy Spirit. As Jesus said to the woman of the well, when we learn to drink living water, we will not be thirsty for earthly substitutions any more (see John 4:14).

Boasting in the Lord is often a sign of being filled with the Holy Spirit and being given divine strength to speak out the light and truth of God in a dark land or to a dark sky. Many prophets in the Scriptures would burst out in glorious worship, boasting about their God in the face of enemy threats. King David is a very good example of this. His psalms can go from asking for help to suddenly extolling his mighty King! The result of divine help was a spontaneous roar of thanksgiving and glory ascending to the Lord.[4]

Good boasts are fitting in the church assembly. We must recognize that the one who is the most interested in what we speak is God Himself. But next to Him are also angels, as well as satan and his demons. They are all affected when they hear people declaring the glory of God. Therefore, we widen our perspective when we come together as one Body before the Lord and declare to all things, visible and invisible, *Who* is worthy of our praise.

It is interesting that women are noted warriors in this area in the Scriptures. They were led by the Holy Spirit to affirm the miracles and kindnesses they experienced by loud proclamations and courageous statements of their faith in God. In so doing, they took a stand and drove a *stake of truth* into their land and for the work of God. Read the songs of Miriam and of Deborah, the praise of Hannah, and the exultation of Mary. I especially like Hannah, who said, *"My mouth boasts over my enemies, for I delight in Your deliverance"* (1 Sam. 2:1). Her enemies were the same that we could face any day for the Lord: the taunts of a rival, the ridicule of culture, and projected shame on womanhood. God defeated them for her. She looked her enemies in the eyes, those who tormented her, and said: "Where is your strength—you have no power against *my* God!" She rose to her full stature in the victory He brought her and trampled her enemies. We will do the same, according to the promises of Psalm 149:6-9 and 44:4-8.

Making our boast in the power of God will strengthen us and make us rise to defeat our enemies. We show that our confidence and trust is in Him, and we stay humble and dependent on His help. We have nothing to boast about in ourselves, but boasting in Him puts us on high and makes us able to trample our enemies under foot. To boast in the Lord is to bring our foot down to crush the lies and the power of our enemies.

There will be a tremendous breakthrough in the worship watch at times through one person raising his or her voice and starting to extol the greatness of God. Boasting boosts our confidence in the Lord and brings encouragement to the whole Body. Boasting is a direction setter. Like geese flying in the ease of the lead goose that breaks through the wind, so a man or a woman who leads the way in extolling the Lord breaks through the spiritual air and frees others to follow. Proclaiming our complete trust in the Lord and speaking of what He has done sets the eyes of God's people on Him, and that is when the scales of our eyes start falling off and we start seeing the invisible realms. Very often, we are then ushered into the joy of the Holy Spirit and to new levels of revelation.

After looking at both evil and good boasting, we can set down a general guideline for understanding boasts. *Evil boasting is to try to rob God of His glory*, and it is an arrogance that will be brought low (see Rom. 11:17-21; Isa. 10:12; 1 Sam. 2:3). *Good boasting means to glory in, rejoice, and proclaim the Lord, His attributes, and His deeds* (see 1 Sam. 2:3), and it builds hope and encouragement. We can learn to discern the source of a boast through what kind of response it generates (its fruit); does it produce fear and intimidation, or courage and rejoicing?

What do you say—shall we make some bold boasts and elevate the Lord this week? *Who is worthy?* Say it again!

PERSONAL REFLECTION

1. What things do I know about God's character and ways from experience, not just hearing? What truths about Him are so cemented into my heart that I would stake my life on their validity?

2. Do I fear the Lord and respect His power and majesty? (Test: If I fell into sin, would I fear people's or God's verdict the most?)

3. To what degree am I comfortable presenting myself before the Lord? What do I have trouble doing to show my heart and my love to Him? If I had the courage, what expressions of worship would I love to develop (dancing, jumping, declaring, raising my hands, and so forth)?

4. Read Isaiah 61:10, Jeremiah 9:23-24, 1 Samuel 17:45-47, and Acts 4:8-13. If I were to boast in the Lord, what would I proclaim, and to whom would I proclaim it?

ENDNOTES

1. Part of a prophetic word at a prayer conference I attended.

2. This picture could refer to Him being resolved to deal with those opposing His rule, which is often what we pray for in our worship watches. As we see from Matthew 25:32-33, He puts the accepted on His right and the rejected on His left.

3. In *Understanding the Dreams You Dream* (Shippensburg, PA: Treasure House, 1993), Ira Milligan shares the biblical keys for interpreting colors. The meaning of colors will be the same for anything pertaining to God's Kingdom, for it is His heavenly language. There is a root meaning for each color, and then there are branch-meanings. I will only share the root meaning and a few branch meanings here, and refer you to this book for a more complete picture. *Black* stands for lack, but also for sin, evil, and mourning. *Blue* means spiritual and also divine revelation or visitation. Dark blue is for God's Spirit, while light blue stands for the human spirit or an evil spirit. *Brown* means dead, but it can also stand for repented or born again. *Gray* stands for "not defined" and vague; it also stands for deception or hidden and false. *Green* stands for mortal life, for immaturity and renewal, while the evergreen stands for eternal life. *Orange* signifies danger or harm. *Pink* means flesh and can also mean either sensual (hot pink) or innocence and chaste (baby pink). *Purple* means royal; it also means noble and majestic. *Red* stands for passion, but can also mean emotion, anger, hatred, enthusiasm, or zeal. White means pure, also spotless, true, and innocent. *Yellow*, finally, means gift (from God), but it can also mean honor, fear, or cowardliness. It is important to know what we are saying—holding up gray and bright pink banners in church or wearing orange robes might not be the best idea!

4. Good examples of such boasting are the deliverance at the Red Sea (see Exod. 14:29-15:18), the victory of Deborah and Barak (see Judg. 4:23-5:5), and the song of Hannah (see 1 Sam. 1:27-2:10). The song of Mary is found in Luke 1:46-55.

CHAPTER EIGHT

THE TAMBOURINE II

THE POWER OF UNITY

It is a wonderful thing to worship the Lord in private. The intimacy of finding a place where there is no need to put up a front is a great treasure, and it is often where the Lord meets our needs. But from the platform of personal devotion we move into the corporate worship. It may be just you and a friend, a small group, a public meeting, or a full-size congregation. The size is not the important thing; the important thing is to come together before Him (see Matt. 18:19-20).

The Lord loves unity. It is not about uniformity; it is about the bonds of love being strong enough to allow for divine, creative diversity. Yet, in the midst of diverse expressions, we display *one in heart and mind* (see Acts 4:32).

Jesus is the center. All believers stand around Him, but according to our walk with Him, we are farther away or closer to Him. The farther away we are, the more discord and sinful attitudes are at work. We have not found our "center of gravity" in Him yet, and the distance between believers is also greater. But the closer we get to Jesus, the closer we also draw to one another. The closer we are to Him, the more He corrects our faulty views and quiets our urge to look critically at one another. The more we look at Him, the more we enjoy each other, all of us receiving His mind on what matters. Where He is, peace reigns.

When we overcome the need to compare and criticize one another and instead begin to love, unity becomes dynamic. Not only do unbelievers shake their heads in amazement and realize that order and stability comes from divine love rather than organization, but we ourselves are blessed by the Lord, who has bound Himself to bless and pour out fresh anointing when we stand together.

> *How good and pleasant it is when brothers live together in unity! It is like precious oil poured on the head, running down on the beard, running down on Aaron's beard, down upon the collar of his robes. It is as if the due of Hermon were falling on Mount Zion. For there the Lord bestows [commands] His blessing, even life forevermore* (Psalm 133).

Oil represents anointing. It also speaks of the presence of the Holy Spirit. Are we not desperate to receive more of the anointing and flow of the Spirit in our lives? It starts with a renewed love for our spiritual family, our brothers and sisters.

Jesus is the head of the priestly order. The anointing He carries as a priest starts flowing down onto His Body (us!) when we are in unity, and we are empowered to serve in our royal priesthood with His authority, with great revelation, and with power to intercede for others with astounding results.

Many times we saw this anointing take place in our team life. We all came from our homes, some sleepy, others stressed, others unwell. The information time ended and we entered worship. The first song would not always bring everybody to a place of worship, but one by one we started entering in to His presence—our eyes stayed on Him, the glorious King. The ripple effect of this communion upward spread as team members would start receiving things from the Lord. One would speak a word or Scripture, another would confirm the same word or had the same sense. Once we had confirmation from the Lord, we could start hitting the target with prayer or be able to take in the presence of the Lord and receive from Him. We strengthened each other to become mighty in our task.

This unity and ability to hear from the Lord corporately greatly helps us in our quest to know the Lord's will and direction. Let me share a story.

In the '90s, while two men of a non-government organization were stationed in Kabul, Afghanistan, they had powerful team times. They became so attuned to the Lord's directions and quiet voice that they numerous times heard the same word or knew what the other one would be sharing. While praying with closed eyes, one would suddenly know, "Yes, my brother has something from the Lord." And right after that the other man would speak up and deliver a word.

During one of those years, the harshness of winter had caused a terrible situation of refugees outside of Herat, the border city into Iran. The two men prayed and felt they should make a two or three day trip to the site and ask the Lord whether they should involve themselves or not. As they got there, they saw the situation. The next morning, they had their breakfast and went to prayer. The leader of the two took out his Bible and said, "I have a Scripture to share." The younger man looked at him and said, "Yes, it is from First Samuel 17, right? The Lord just told me the book and the chapter. I believe we are to work here in Herat. And I actually feel that I am supposed to move here with my wife." After further prayer and confirmation from the Lord to start a work in Herat, the two men left to return to Kabul. The younger man said to his friend, "God will already have told my wife. Don't say anything to her. You will see."

As the plane landed, they found her waiting for them, despite the fact that she had not received any news of when they would be arriving. She went up to them and asked, "So, how was the trip?" The younger man tried to look nonchalant as he answered, "Oh, it was OK." His wife said, "Yes? The Lord told me that we were going to move there." How clear, how awesome His leading is when watered with prayer and worship!!

There are some things the Lord will only reveal in a group setting. When we are alone, we many times come to the Lord for our own edification and having our needs met. That is how it should be. Other people have the gift of intercession and pray on behalf of others. But the group setting is where we start *forming ranks*. We are not there to do it all on our own, filling all spots at once. Instead we become effective and joyful in having a part in a greater mission. These group missions are very fulfilling, mostly because we move beyond our own needs and interests and start serving the Father's heart for the lost and, therefore, share in His joy. It is exciting to have a part in accomplishing something bigger than what could be done as individual believers.

When we join together to pray and worship, the heart of the Lord surfaces. As we bring all our puzzle pieces together, we start determining with greater accuracy, with the help of *two or three witnesses* (impressions), what the Lord wants.

Another aspect of the anointing that surfaces in a team worship situation is the emerging of spiritual gifts. The gifts were given for the building up of the Body of believers (see 1 Cor. 12:7). Therefore, when we gather together to hear from the Lord, we will usually have a display of these gifts. Prophetic words, healings, wisdom, words of knowledge, and the discerning of spirits are there to be put in action to strengthen the believers. What an awesome ministry we do for each other as we listen to His voice!

Finally, group worship establishes God's throne and rule in the geographical area where it is being offered up. This is a major group assignment in which we battle "the prince of the *powers* of the air," satan and his greater principalities. It is not meant to be tackled by lone rangers. It is the anointing of unity that breaks through the dark gates of these demonic strongholds. Worship and fasting are major keys for breakthrough in this area. We must do the "smaller part" of just presenting ourselves as worshipers of God and let Him move the darkness. The more focused we are on Him, the less the enemy has a chance to attack us with fear and intimidation. We form ranks, but mostly we just stand our ground until He Himself makes the enemy camp fall apart. In fact, there are few things as scary for a demon as when we blow trumpets (worship) and march (obey) with the intent of breakthrough, as at Jericho. They fear Him!

I want us to look at Islam for a moment. In many ways Muslims move and act as an army—but of course against the Lord, not for Him. But pay attention to the times we are in, and notice how they work. While the West (the Christian world) by their own hands embraced small family sizes, the Muslim world always encouraged large families, especially sons. They live, eat, speak, dream, and chant their creeds with every aspect of their lives. They worship five times a day. They enforce the outward expression of worship and submission to Allah, the very same thing the Lord so desires from *our* hearts. In the heavenlies, the big ongoing attention is focused on who will receive worship. Muslims know what they are doing, and they speak of it openly: they are on Jihad, Holy War, against anything that will raise itself against their religion. They are an army in the way they talk and act.

The oppression and the darkness this kind of devotion creates can not be broken through without major spiritual force. It is beyond what any of us could wield. But in Zechariah 4:6 the Lord gives us His answer, *"Not by might, nor by power, but by My Spirit, says the Lord Almighty."* The Lord Himself will dissolve the darkness of the skies if we remember to lift Him up. We need to exalt our Commander. We need to set our attention on what *He* will do, not so much on what we should do. We need to stand in His presence and wait on Him, as long as it takes, until He gives us keys to unlock our areas. It is all in Him, with Him, for Him, and through Him that every obstacle will be overcome.

The power of unity puts the odds so overwhelmingly in our favor that satan will do all he can to keep us from it; and the primary way he uses is *disunity*. While being in a close-knit team of a dozen people, we experienced this continually. Although we experienced great highs in some of the meetings, on the side we struggled with pride, the need to be seen, unforgiveness, eccentricity, sickness, depression, and leadership issues. Some attacks were

formed on the natural dislikes of personalities; others came as misunder-
standings, differences in opinions, and finally accusations that set off chain
reactions of suspicion. We were hit so hard that our bonds of trust were
severed, and although we were all committed to worship, our strength of
unity waned.

I share this with you so that you may realize that satan does not play
fair. When we start standing together and causing damage to what he has
built, he gets incensed and forms schemes to stop us. It is our love for one
another and for the Lord that keeps us standing in such times. When we
are targeted we must lift our heads and realize that our enemy is threatened
enough to start defending something that is precious to him. That in itself is
confirmation that we are part of something important. Let us not give way,
but anchor ourselves deeper in those days, with great resolve to love and
forgive every insult, unkindness, and misunderstanding. Actively repenting
and seeking forgiveness will bring about greater glory and anointing than
we had before the attack came against us. *Do not let the enemy have his day
with you. Let his schemes fall flat, for the Lord is about to break through in your
midst!*

LEAVING CONSTANTINE BEHIND

Do you remember Constantine? We talked about him briefly in Chapter Three. He was the Christian emperor who turned Christianity into an
accepted religion. The sudden truce after horrific martyrdom saw a surge
of new converts; churches quickly went up, as did stability and the beginning of traditional church functions. *Constantine is the name of the demon
principality that oversees organized Christian religion and loves the façade of
spirituality, but denies the power of Jesus* (see 2 Tim. 3:5).

We are humans with a strong urge to put down roots. We quickly set up
habits, ruts, and traditions to capture what is precious or a priority in our
lives and make it part of us. We do it in hundreds of different ways—going
to the same grocery store, sitting in our favorite chair, keeping our seats in

the church year after year, having that same, special dessert every Thanksgiving. The ruts keep us organized and efficient, and we feel at home. When we enter a new stage or move to a new location, a lot of patterns and familiar ways are rooted up and have to find new paths. It is time-consuming and tiring to put down new roots.

When it comes to our lives as Christians, our strongest roots must be in Jesus. It is not in *something,* but in Someone. When our roots are in Him, then when He moves, we are able to follow, and when He introduces new things, we are not overwhelmed. Our *home* in Him is not moved by changing location or trying something new. Although we feel the changes and have to make adjustments to new scenarios, we are not root-less. Our stability is in the Immovable Rock. Indeed, the Lord says that there will be times of great turmoil on earth, and He promises to be the stability for our time (see Isa. 33:6).

Worship is one of the biggest areas of our lives where our roots must be firmly placed in Him. The Holy Spirit must be allowed to lead, or our work as worshipers will greatly suffer. For example, if we are comforted by a certain style of music, it may start putting down roots in our hearts so that when music is not played the way we like, we get offended and shut off spiritually. It should be a sign to us that our roots are not in the right place. Wherever we sense the presence of the Holy Spirit, there we should be able to worship. We may not enjoy the beat or the noise level, but we can still stand and give Him glory.

Constantine symbolizes organized religion, predictability, and comfort—this spirit is the quencher of the inner promptings of the Holy Spirit. The Lord is a genius at putting our faith to the test. He gives us tests that physically are as easy as a child's game to obey, but hard for our egos to carry out. Has the Lord ever told you to ask forgiveness of someone you have not seen for years? It is such a simple thing to do, but our pride and embarrassment make it a real hurdle. *Nah, she wouldn't even remember! I will look like an idiot! What will those around say?* Has He ever prompted you to go up to someone to pray for them or lay your arm around their shoulder? When He speaks, our flesh tends to clamp up and resist immediately.

The beauty of worship from the heart, leaving tradition and facades behind, is that it makes room for the work of God to take place, even in the midst of the singing and the praise. In churches where the worship time is predictable and follows a pattern, a time schedule, or other formats, it is most of the time inappropriate to be spontaneous or suddenly go and do what the Spirit might say. The institution, the church, then becomes a hurdle, not a motivator, for obedience. *That* is the desire of the spirit of constantine.

Because we as humans love the safety of predictability and order, it is easy for a church to rein in the corporate worship time and set up perimeters for its time frame and its expression. But who do we come to worship? The Lord. What kind of worshipers is He seeking? Jesus said He seeks those who worship in *spirit* and in truth (see John 4:23). To be able to worship we must have the Holy Spirit, and He must be in charge. He will not come and do His work unless He is welcomed in and given space to move. And once He moves, there needs to be room for Him to do His desire. The worship time is meant to give God glory and build for Him a throne from which He reigns.

The task of the people who lead worship is much more than conducting music. They are the ministers who promote the flow of true adoration ascending, and they discern and make room for the Lord to move among His people. They *lead* God's people into His presence. The work of a worship leader is carried out not by talent, but by anointing.

It sometimes takes time to come to a place of worship. We have to lay down the busyness of our minds and quiet our hearts. As we do that, our true condition rises to the surface—our untended hurts, our insecurities or fears, and our deepest longings. We are faced with the choice of either putting on a good front for the sake of appearance or being willing to be vulnerable before God and those around us. If we have not dealt with our sins or spiritual needs, they will show up in worship. The Holy Spirit knows that they must be dealt with before we can stand and minister. Constantine opposes this healing and the freedom it would bring.

Right there in our seats the pressure is on: constantine, the enemy, wants us to keep it down and out of sight. *Be respectable. You will look like a fool. People in your position in the church cannot show they have these kinds of problems.* The Lord wants us to spill our contents before Him. *Give me your burden, and I will heal you. I already know of your sins and have provided for them. Give Me your stress and your anxiety. I will be your Peace.*

As we run to the Lord in repentance and trust, He heals us. Spiritual surgery is a messy business; different people, with different backgrounds and different problems, manifest the touch of God in different ways; there are wails, tears, groans, and loud cries in the room. While some are still in this process of being emptied, others are being healed and filled with joy—they are now manifesting His presence with laughter, singing, and dancing. Real life is happening now, to the bewilderment or delight of some and to the offense of others. But the Lord is pleased. He is receiving true worship, and He has met with many of His children and tended to their wounds. For Him it was a good worship time!

We must let Him have us, all there is. If a format enhances our fellowship with the Lord, then it is serving well. But the format is not to become a dictator of the expressions of the people of God. In our worship the Holy Spirit is Lord—He is free to move as He pleases in His house, and we are free to move with Him. And constantine will have to move over.

EXTRAVAGANT LOVE

In the Scriptures we will find that there were times when the Lord was especially moved by a gesture of love toward Him. I have decided to call this *Extravagant Love.* The Lord seems to say, *"You are Mine. When you give beyond the ordinary to please Me, when you show the depth of your love, you win Me over. I want to spill My love over you and over thousands in return."*

You can not fake it to see if it will work. But you can decide to give your very being, your extravagant love, to Him. He will receive you with pleasure!

These are some examples of extravagant love in Scripture.

Solomon showed his love for the Lord by walking according to the statutes of his father David, except that he offered sacrifices and burned incense on the high places. The king went to Gibeon to offer sacrifices, for that was the most important high place, and Solomon offered a thousand burnt offerings on that altar. At Gibeon the Lord appeared to Solomon during the night in a dream, and God said, "Ask for whatever you want Me to give you" (1 Kings 3:3-5).

A thousand animals, paid for just to be sacrificed—God never required such amounts; they were not necessary. *Such waste, Solomon, such extravagance in your display of love and loyalty.* Yet in return the Lord granted him whatever he wished. The Lord took notice of him.

Here's another story of extravagance.

While Jesus was in Bethany in the home of a man known as Simon the Leper, a woman came to Him with an alabaster jar of very expensive perfume, which she poured on His head as He was reclining at the table. When the disciples saw this, they were indignant. "Why this waste?" they asked. "This perfume could have been sold at a high price and the money given to the poor." Aware of this, Jesus said to them, "Why are you bothering this woman? She has done a beautiful thing to Me... I tell you the truth, wherever this gospel is preached throughout the world, what she has done will also be told in memory of her" (Matthew 26:6-13).

Extravagance is generally misunderstood and looked at as a waste. But when it comes to showing your love for the Lord, it is beautiful to Him. He gave the woman a place of honor in history. She is not the hidden, no-name woman who saw Jesus. She is the one who gave the best she had just to say, "I find You better than the best I have, Lord. I choose *You.* I love *You.*"

Now let's look at David.

At that time David was in the stronghold, and the Philistine garrison was at Bethlehem. David longed for water and said, "Oh, that someone would get me a drink of water from the well near the gate of Bethlehem!" So the three mighty men broke through the Philistine lines, drew water from the well near the gate of Bethlehem and carried it back to David. But he refused to drink it; instead, he poured it out before the Lord. "Far be it from me, O Lord, to do this!" he said. "Is it not the blood of men who went at the risk of their lives?" And David would not drink it (2 Samuel 23:14-17).

David had the love of his soldiers. They were so devoted that they were willing to risk their lives to satisfy a desire of his, although not a necessary one—they could have found water elsewhere. But because the king was attached to his ancestral town, they were willing to go there—for him. As soon as they got back with the precious water, David realized that their sacrifice was bigger than he could accept. The extravagance of their love had only one worthy recipient: the Lord. He was not ungrateful here by not drinking: he simply joined their extravagance and gave what he treasured most to the One he loved most. It was that kind of heart that God loved in David, and because of it He promised him that he would be the beginning of the eternal kingship (see 2 Sam. 7:16).

In these days there is a surge among believers to get back to this kind of love. One part of this movement has received the name *Ministering to Jesus*. It is the kind of worship that goes beyond the declaring, proclaiming, making noise to the Lord; it is the quiet, simple adoration at His feet, offering up the precious fragrance of surrender, lives laid bare before Him. As a result, these kinds of gatherings and individuals have tales to tell of God's extravagant outpourings in return.

In the spring of 2001, Afghanistan was in a hopeless state. The Taliban had managed to quench all joy, all music, and all happy play of the people. Thousands of widows, with no permission to work and no way to support their children, were starving in the city of Kabul. Any little sign of discontentment or diversion from their strict laws (such as a certain length of a man's beard or a woman showing her ankle or wrist) meant imprisonment at the least and many times death. In addition to this, the country was going on its third year of drought.

In the States, some women who practiced this *Ministering to Jesus* heard His call to go to Kabul and to worship there for six days. They would be the physical presence, backed by a quarter of a million intercessors. One amazing band of intercessors was in an Argentinean prison. The Lord had miraculously saved two thousand inmates out of the three thousand that were incarcerated there, and a thousand had committed themselves to becoming intercessors for the world. They now joined to pray for Kabul.

The Lord had said there would be six women worshiping, but after much praying, they still left the States as a group of four. In Pakistan another woman joined the prayer team, and as they came onto the scene, their sixth woman, a lady from Germany who worked in the city, joined them.

How strange—a few women, spending day and night in a room in Kabul for a week, doing "nothing" to alleviate the plight of a suffering city, but coming with the one goal in mind: to show their extravagant love for Jesus in one of the most oppressive countries of the world.

I happened to be in the city at this time, and for one night I joined these women. It was my first experience of seeing this kind of worship. Nobody sang; nobody talked. Carefully selected songs and words were projected with an overhead onto a whitewashed wall. The women were still, some prostrating themselves, others kneeling, some sitting, one silently managing the overheads. There was nothing extraordinary in the way it was presented. Yet it was a full-time, lavish gift of time and love sent up to Almighty God from a place of darkness.

And so they worshiped. The Lord had said to worship for six days. It so happened that they started on the day of the Afghan New Year, Nau Roz, which literally means "a new day." An Afghan believer later told them that there was evidence that Nau Roz was originally a Christian festival that was celebrated for six days paralleling the six days of creation. While they were worshiping, the ladies sensed that they were planting for the Lord a garden where He could rest and walk with His children—just as He, after the six days of creation, had finished the first garden!

On the sixth day of worship, they finished their last watch at 10 P.M. At 11 P.M. it started to rain. Through the night it poured and poured, and for the next days it rained off and on. The drought broke. The Lord was so pleased with His new garden, the place prepared for His pleasure, that He watered it and the whole country with it!

When the ladies left the country and entered Pakistan, they found an Afghan Christian woman who told them of a dream she had had. She had seen six women shut up in a house in Kabul, praying and worshiping—and then a huge storm lifting off the city. The prayer team was the first layer of the fulfillment of this dream. Half a year later, six foreign ladies were arrested by the Taliban, one of them this same German woman who had joined the worship watch. Now they worshiped in their forced seclusion for three months before their miraculous rescue, when the dark cloud of the Taliban regime lifted for good.

What the Lord did for Afghanistan, with millions of people around the world praying and watching the news, is to me one of the most vivid testimonies of God's power and sovereignty in our day. It may well be that God could have done all that He did with simply people interceding around the world. Instead He chose a small band of people and their extravagant show of love to be a channel of His divine answer.

The woman in charge of this adventure in Kabul would like to state, in regards to the *Ministering to Jesus*, that they do not regard this as a form of spiritual warfare. The goal is not really breakthrough, although the Lord many times is willing to just give it as a gift. The goal is to be with Jesus and to adore Him. It is a part of the worship experience that can radically change our perspective on life.

WATCHMEN ON THE WALL

One day I was talking to a friend of mine. She was sharing with me how her job of ministering to very needy people left her emotionally very drained. I encouraged her to seek out time to worship the Lord and be rejuvenated by Him. That night I had this dream.

I was looking into a festive party with many people gathered in a room, walking around. A group of men were talking among themselves and then chose a young, beautiful girl in a veil to help them in a secret, undercover operation. She was asked to build a wall through dancing. Then in the dream, the people all sat down, with the girl in the center. No one noticed how she quietly and skillfully moved her feet in dance while sitting, and a wall was being built in front of her. It was a three-sided small wall, like the beginning of a watchtower. No one noticed the wall going up either. The girl was very skillful and knowledgeable in how she built. Then I woke up.

I looked up the Biblical meaning of some of the things I had dreamed. The primary meaning of *dance* is "worship"; *feet* means "heart," and *wall* stands for "barrier" or "defense." The Lord was encouraging my friend to begin to practice the art of worship. He in return would see that it would work as a defense in her own life against the stresses she met and that she would be able to step up into her "watch tower" and start seeing what happened around her with clearer spiritual perspective and sight.

When we do not see the spiritual reality, it is hard to invoke change. But worship is truly a wonderful asset the Lord has given us to raise us to new levels of insight and vision. We become watchmen who take our stand between Heaven and earth. We worship and touch His heart, and we receive impressions of what we should ask for; we ask, and He acts—and all this as we simply soak in the presence of our God and praise Him!

In the book of Ezekiel we find the Lord expressing His desire for someone to stand in the gap to restrain His righteous judgment and provoke His mercy:

I looked for a man among them who would build up the wall and stand before Me in the gap on behalf of the land so I would not have to destroy it, but I found none. So I will pour out My wrath on them and consume them with My fiery anger, bringing down on their own heads all they have done, declares the Sovereign Lord (Ezekiel 22:30-31).

There are many examples in Scripture of the Lord looking for a spokesman and withholding His judgment because someone pleaded for mercy on someone else's behalf—Abraham for Sodom, Jesus on the cross, and Stephen for his persecutors, as well as many Old Testament prophets. *I will stand at my watch and station myself on the ramparts; I will look to see what He will say to me...* (Hab. 2:1).

One morning in our team meetings the Lord very graciously allowed me to see this wall. I had spoken out the Scripture above, waiting for the Lord to speak to us and let us know what to pray for, when I suddenly found myself on the wall. It was about three feet thick and maybe two or three miles high. Wow! I saw my team members standing beside me in our worship room and at the same time on the wall. It seemed as if I could feel the breeze, and being so high up, I had no desire to move. *Why am I here, suspended between Heaven and earth? Oh, yes, I am the Lord's watchman who stands in the gap. What shall I ask for, Lord?* I let my eyes dwell on the land below. I knew the people down there—their poverty, their struggles with corruption, and their mindless obedience to Allah while their spiritual leaders exploited and used them to remain in power. I pitied their hopeless state.

"Lord, they need shepherds. Good shepherds who will not lead them astray. Oh, Lord, that they would know You as their Shepherd."

I did not know what else to pray for, so I fell silent, still standing on that wall. Then my leader's wife spoke, with wonder in her voice.

"I see a mosque from above. The people are bowing down to worship. But Jesus is walking among them, and He is touching some of their heads!" The Lord was already moving in response to our prayers.

What we do in intercession is real. When we enter into God's presence to stand in the gap for people and places, we are priests, anointed to represent them before His throne. It is an awesome privilege, and history will change its course because of it. God has set us far above our human position and granted us a place before Him as watchmen. We are in a wonderful position of bringing God's mercy to others.

While the world runs after idols of all kinds, we worship the one true God who says,

> *You shall not make for yourself an idol in the form of anything in heaven above or on the earth beneath or in the waters below. You shall not bow down to them and worship them; for I, the Lord your God, am a jealous God, punishing the children for the sin of the fathers to the third and fourth generation of those who hate Me, but showing love [mercy] to a thousand generations of those who love Me and keep My commandments* (Exodus 20:4-6).

Here the worshiper of God is set in contrast to the idolater. The ungodly make their descendants inherit curses, but those who set their hearts on loving and worshiping the Lord find themselves channels of love and mercy to countless people far into the future! His divine love and mercy will spill out and touch many because of the worship He receives from just one true worshiper. This is a powerful reminder that as we worship we are agents of mercy. Just as Abraham interceded and bargained for the godless city of Sodom, so do those who seek the Lord's face find themselves in a position where the Lord is inviting them to plead mercy where He otherwise must pour out judgment.

God loves to show mercy to His children and to extend it to the lost and ungodly. Ecclesiastes 9:14-15 shares this:

> *There was once a small city with only a few people in it. And a powerful king came against it, surrounded it and built huge siegeworks against it. Now there lived in that city a man poor*

but wise, and he saved the city by his wisdom. But nobody re-membered that poor man.

In a similar way do we become agents of mercy for our regions. Although no one may know our secret efforts to deliver our cities, our pleas of mercy seek out the very wisdom and aid of Almighty God. However strong the demonic strongholds are, we still have wisdom (Jesus Himself, the wisdom of God) on our side. God can, and will, bring about mercy for many if we spend time in worship!

PERSONAL REFLECTION

1. Have I found a group of people to worship with on a deeper level, where I sense the Lord's presence? If not, where could I go to do this?

2. Have I ever given anything to the Lord that was costly for me personally? What happened after that, showing that the Lord was pleased with my love gift?

3. Do I have any religious traditions in my family that seem to be more an obstacle than a help in my pursuit of loving God? What could I do to break with the spirit of religiosity?

4. What do I feel the Lord calling me to do the most—praying for individuals, for geographic areas or countries, for my own nation and its government, or for the Church? What has He said to me that makes me know that this is part of what He has called me to do as a watchman?

5. What part of worship makes me feel the most joyful and energized—the personal intercession, quiet adoration, proclamation, prophetic input, or something else? What could I do to train myself to become excellent on my part of the watchman's wall?

CHAPTER NINE

PURITY

CASTING DOWN THE IDOLS OF OUR FATHERS

Listen, O daughter, consider and give ear: forget your people and your father's house. The King is enthralled by your beauty; honor Him, for He is your Lord (Psalm 45:10-11).

This passage is not merely about a girl chosen to be the wife of a king. This Psalm is talking about us and Jesus, the King of kings. He chose us to be His Bride, and we have agreed to be His. In return for this pledge of marriage to Him (that will take place in Heaven at the Wedding Supper of the Lamb, the ultimate covenant between God and His people, see Rev. 19:7), He asks us to prepare ourselves. We must be set apart; we must be purified; we must go through a beautification process to become ready for our heavenly Husband. This chapter describes some of the purification process and identifies areas in our lives that need to be made clean.

The first beckoning from our Lover is to get away from our past and to set our hearts on the future He is preparing for us. Our identity cannot be in what has been, the circumstances that shaped our experience, or our family ties. We must forget what we were to become what we are meant to be.

This was vividly portrayed to me when I married a man of another nation and had to turn my back on all that was familiar from my home country. I gave away most of my books and let go of my music to start a new collection we could both enjoy. I had to forget about the foods I was used to and learn to enjoy the foods of my new land. I made the transition from Swedish humor and speech to the American Midwest drawl (I had to! The people would not even give me water until I learned to say it right! *Wudder...*). Although some of the letting go was painful, the Lord made up for it in amazing ways. I embraced Psalm 45:10 as the Lord's promise to be with me and His confirmation that He desired this change.

To forget our father's house is not the same as to abandon our family! We are commanded to honor our father and mother (see Exod. 20:12). The difference is that before our parents were our guides and trainers in how to manage life. They acted; we imitated. They said; we believed. They pronounced, and that is how it was. The nourishment they gave, whether positive or negative, went into our lifeblood. We become more like our parents every year. Now, though, our life has been planted in God, and He pumps His blood into our beings. Whatever is not good in us, He wants to wash away. And that is why He says to us, *"Listen, forget your country and your father's house."* We are used to going to our old sources for water, but we must learn to drink from Him now. Our instinctive training by earthly teachers has come to an end; now we must learn to listen directly to the Master.

The Lord set our parents above us, to train us for a season, and most of them did what they could to care for us and to help us in the right direction (I wouldn't trade mine for anything!). But whether our parents were good, ignorant, or wicked in their dealings with us, the Lord wants the past to go so that His new life for us can have its chance to prepare us for the throne. There are many evil things that make its way through our family lines: curses, traditions, and idols. The Lord does not want the sins of our fathers to keep us from our destiny. That is why He does not give His final training of us over to anyone but the Holy Spirit. No one but this Heavenly Trainer can help us discern truth and deliver us into complete freedom.

In Judges 6 we read about Gideon's encounter with the Lord and his call to redeem Israel. Before Gideon was allowed to start his work, though, the Lord commanded him to tear down the idols of Baal and Asherah in his father's compound and to build an altar to the Lord in its place. Though he was afraid of what the reaction of his countrymen would be, he obeyed. These two idols were worshiped and sacrificed to in the most perverse and wicked ways of institutionalized child sacrifice and prostitution. This was the environment in which Gideon had grown up, and the Lord was saving him through his obedience.

What is in our backgrounds? Whatever took place or was allowed by our parents, grandparents, and great grandparents, it is worth knowing. Unless there was repentance and deliverance, it is in some way still affecting us and having a hold on our lives (see Deut. 5:9). We did not ask for this baggage, but that is the strength of the bonds between us and our family. You may struggle with stronger temptations than others have because it was allowed in your family—alcoholism, violence and anger, manipulation, sexual perversion, witchcraft, rebellion, suicidal thoughts, unfaithfulness with work or family, and so forth. Our family ties pull us toward a similar destiny as our fathers, for good or bad. Our salvation is our escape to break from our past and to renounce all evil influence on our lives (which is done through specific prayers that mention names, actions, and words).[1] The blood of Jesus is ready to heal and cleanse us.

Hebrews 12:1-2 admonishes us to throw off everything that hinders in our pursuit of God's will for our lives. We are not meant to stay under the yoke of sin. We are meant to be free and whole. We are meant to be pure and holy. We are meant for Jesus, the Bridegroom.

WITH ALL OUR MINDS

Jesus replied, "'Love the Lord your God with all your heart and with all your soul and with all your mind.' This is the first and greatest commandment" (Matthew 22:37).

In our search for purity we frequently stumble, not because our actions are sinful, but because we have not trained our minds to be obedient to the Lord. Previously, we read that Jesus saw it as of primary importance to love the Lord our God with our minds. I believe the mind is one of the greatest obstacles to a wholehearted pursuit of God and to hearing and obeying the quiet voice of the Holy Spirit.

Our minds and thoughts are directly linked to the condition of our hearts and their deep desires (see Rom. 8:5; Matt. 15:19). But our hearts, according to Jeremiah 17:9, cannot be trusted; they are desperately wicked and deceive us. All humankind is in bondage to a carnal mind, a mind that produces *death*, until the Holy Spirit is allowed to rule it (see Rom. 8:4-9). Even when humankind wants what is *good*, it still produces death—it is only the Lord Himself, who is Life, who can produce life. Even after a person is saved and receives a new identity, the mind is not instantly regenerated. It has to be retrained and submitted to the voice of the Spirit and the Word of God.

Through salvation we receive new hearts; the Holy Spirit starts redirecting the desires of our hearts and purifying our motives. We come to love the Lord and desire more things in line with His will. But our hearts are not the only battle for our minds. The next onslaught is from the world.

We must remember our beginning. We ate of the wrong tree. We ate "knowledge" instead of life. The mind craves knowledge; it wants to know everything, anything. It feeds on everything that comes its way from the heart, the eyes, the ears, the emotions, and the physical touch. We constantly accumulate knowledge. And through knowledge, we accumulate experience—human wisdom. God says in His Word that this wisdom is not at all helpful—it is earthly, sensual, and sometimes even demonic (see 1 Cor. 3:19; James 3:15).

Human reasoning will not lead to life. It opposes the Lord's counsel and cannot submit itself to God's rule (see Rom. 8:7). Therefore, *our minds must not rule our decisions and our lives.*

For all of us who tend to think a great deal, the Lord will have to bring our minds into submission to His leading or we become useless for service. This becomes an excellent training ground for learning how to trust the Lord in all areas of our lives. If we can lay down our own reasoning and instead submit it to the Lord's voice, we start recognizing that He knows more than we do, even about ourselves. We find that we can trust Him more than we can trust our own thoughts and conclusions. If such a trust cements itself into our souls, we will then be in a good place to walk the walk of faith like Abraham, who started on a journey without knowing his destination. He simply trusted the God who had called him.

Jesus operated by the Spirit, not by reasoning. While He and the work the Father had sent Him to do were constantly opposed by the intellectual spiritual leaders of His day, who *reasoned in their hearts,* Jesus *perceived in His spirit* (see Mark 2:6-8). We must come to a place where we accept the fact that God cannot use our intellect until it is completely in submission to His voice. Most of the mind finds its food from the tree of the knowledge of good and evil and bears no good fruit. How many times do we try to solve a spiritual problem by trying to think our way through, just to become more confused than we were in the beginning! Yet, when we seek the Lord, the Spirit gives us His peace and then quietly hands us the solution.

We are responsible to bring our minds to submission to God's truth rather than putting God's Word to the scrutiny of our minds. The more we walk in His light, the more our lives are illumined by revelation and truth. We must not trust our minds—like a willful child, it must be trained to become productive. But once the mind has been subjected to the lordship of Christ, we can become effective thinkers for Him—clear-minded, loving God with all our hearts *and* all our minds, full of divine life and great peace (see Rom. 8:6-7).

RESEARCHING HISTORY

To Adam He said, "Because you listened to your wife and ate from the tree about which I commanded you, 'You must not eat of it,' cursed is the ground because of you; through painful toil you will eat of it all the days of your life..." (Genesis 3:17).

The Lord said [to Cain], "What have you done? Listen! Your brother's blood cries out to Me from the ground. Now you are under a curse and driven from the ground, which opened its mouth to receive your brother's blood from your hand. When you work the ground, it will no longer yield its crops for you. You will be a restless wanderer on the earth" (Genesis 4:10-12).

There are always reasons to why our surroundings are the way they are. The Lord handed the responsibility to care for the earth to humanity; He made us lords. Therefore, by our words and by our actions we decide what our domain will look like.

In Deuteronomy 28 God tells His people that on the one hand, living in obedience to Him brings blessings to us, our descendants, and thousands of others! On the other hand, disobedience to God's commands puts us under a curse, and that curse clings to our family for three and four generations. Our decisions affect not only ourselves, but scores of people *and* our surroundings. Many are concerned about the environment and the balance in nature. We should be even more concerned about our spiritual climate and strive to positively affect the earth through righteous acts.

Because of the effects of past actions on our current situations, we, as the Lord's soldiers, have an opportunity to find the source of some of the trouble around us. We can research history. Some fellow warriors have made it their passion to find and file historical data that point to spiritual bondages or curses passed onto the ground; these people are known as *spiritual mappers*. Their collected data and ability to pinpoint spiritual sources can save an intercessor or warrior much time and effort.

As we saw from the Lord's words to Adam, his disobedience transferred as a curse onto the ground, making it unresponsive and hard to work. If *we* can find out what sins or actions have caused *our* surrounding to harden, then we have a way to seek out the Lord in repentance and restoration.

In our day there are records of hundreds of places in the world that have renounced their past wickedness and have seen miraculous restoration of their physical surroundings. Fiji is one such example. Through a series of steps of repentance and reconciliation, some villages suddenly had clean drinking water again after years of pollution, causing dysentery and death, and their lakes came back alive with fish. Even their crops grew larger and better.[2]

What are some things we should look for as we begin researching our areas? Here is a list of six sources of trouble:

1. *Innocent bloodshed.* As in the case of Cain, murder casts a curse on the ground.

2. *Witchcraft and idol worship.* When people give their power to demons, evil and sin will reign. Pay attention to regional symbols, charms, and mascots—they are good clues of spiritual heritages. Look at important buildings, such as capitol buildings and court houses, for insignias and mottos.

3. *Curses and blessings.* If they were important enough to go into writing, they are probably in effect. They are especially significant if they were pronounced by someone in authority in their sphere of spiritual influence, such as a mayor speaking over his city, an Indian chief over his territory, and so forth.

4. *Oppression against the orphan, the widow, the poor, and the helpless.* The Lord takes it very seriously when those who are set to protect, exploit instead. Look for data on children's homes, care of the elderly, and abortion clinics. What has been done for the poor in the area?

5. *Bribes and the subverting of justice.* Find records of court cases, and read biographies of area judges, mayors, and political figures. Usually newspaper articles from past years will highlight scams and misconduct. Find books and articles featuring the history of your city or area.

6. *Racial hatred.* The Lord commands us to be kind toward the alien and the stranger. If there are racial conflicts or tensions in a city, there is likely some incident in the past that stirred up the animosity. Research the background of the people groups settled in the area—when did they come, and how were they received? What heritage did they bring with them?

One area in the Midwest, just a few miles in radius, is very *accident-prone*. It has a history of drug abuse, highway accidents, and accidents while using farm machinery, as well as a high rate of teenagers committing suicide. Could this history of extreme deaths be purely coincidental? It's very unlikely. Whenever we see patterns repeating themselves in a certain location, it is a clue that there has been one or many incidents in its past that have placed the area under a curse. In many cases, there are reconciliation steps that need to be taken between families or peoples before the healing of the land can begin.

Spiritual mapping is not normal research. Many times we do not know what incident or what word helped strongholds be erected in the region. Sometimes we can find patterns and criminal activities circling certain locations, which would be good indicators of the place of origin. Many times we simply have to keep praying and asking the Lord until He sends us information of where the roots are. From reading testimonies and looking at our own experience, we've found that the Lord often takes us through a series of steps, where He only gives us one or two things to pray for at a time. He holds the keys to transformation. He knows what offenses must be removed, what sins must be atoned for, and what wickedness must be confessed and repented of. If we persevere in bringing our land before Him, He will help us disperse the darkness with His light!

IMPURITIES IN OUR CULTURE

Exodus 23:2 says, *"Do not follow the crowd in doing wrong...."* The Lord knows that every culture and people has its own set of rules and folk laws, but He does not want His people to be ignorantly following any and every practice of those around them. We must put our culture to the test.

With culture I do not only mean countries. Culture is the flavor of the spiritual climate we live in, and it generally holds a great degree of influence over our lives. The culture in its smallest form is our home and our immediate family. We have created or been born into a culture that is held in place by those who exercise authority in the home. Culture is in our schools, our churches, our towns or cities, our regions, our countries, and our continents. Therefore, to have a better look at what our culture is, one of the best things we can do is to place ourselves in a new culture and ponder the differences.

To be separated from our home culture can be a very disorienting experience, yet the growth and change that come to a believer through such an experience is tremendous. It is in the emotional vacuum between the lost home and a foreign atmosphere that God often becomes our very sustenance and survival, and He teaches us to live in the world and not of it.

After persevering for more than a year in a foreign setting, most people come out having had their perspective drastically changed. Reentering our own culture again can also be a challenge, but we find that the experience helps us discern the things in our culture that are destructive influences from the enemy from that which is healthy. God has started separating us for Himself. It can be painful and lonely at times, but we are blessed with a new level of awareness of the schemes of our enemy.

A tremendous asset to any church is taking time for missions- and prayer trips. Even if we do not go with the intention to work, it is still a valuable investment if we go to observe and learn what God is doing in the Body of Christ in other nations. If we do not have this kind of opportunity, we can visit different churches in our own country to get a feel for what God is doing and find out where life is flowing. We could also enter peoples' homes with a spiritual alertness, paying attention to differences in traditions and way of life. The same goes for the study of individuals. We try to locate the slogans, the thoughts we hear repeated as popular opinion, and it gives us an indicator of a cultural influence having been adopted. What about ourselves; do we say what everyone else is saying? Do we think along the same lines everyone else is thinking? In that case, what is the message? Our minds are very pliable to outward influence. If we accept popular thoughts with no scrutiny, we are also susceptible to deception and mass delusion. If we train our minds to watch out for what is being propagated, we can consciously throw away the ungodly thoughts and keep what is true.

> *The weapons that we fight with are not the weapons of this world. On the contrary, they have divine power to demolish strongholds. We demolish arguments and every pretension that sets itself up against the knowledge of God, and we take captive every thought to make it obedient to Christ* (2 Corinthians 10:4-5).

A CLEAN HEART

Who may ascend the hill of the Lord? Who may stand in His holy place? He who has clean hands and a pure heart, who does not lift up his soul to an idol or swear by what is false (Psalm 24:3-4).

The desire of our hearts is to be allowed near the King and to hear what He will say. In order to do this, we must have clean hands and a pure heart, as the psalmist declares. But how can people keep clean hearts with a flood of sin and temptation constantly around them? How can we learn to avoid this onslaught of evil and stand clean before God?

The answer is provided by the Lamb of God, who bore our sins on the cross. There is nothing we need to do to obtain a pure heart; it is a free gift made through the trade of Christ's sinless heart, which was condemned and nailed to the cross, for our sinful one. We receive by faith the forgiveness of sins and the gift of a clean heart before our Father. What a priceless gift, and what a sacrifice was made that we might receive it!

Our hearts are easily soiled, though. Our fallen nature is still there. Our minds still have thought patterns from the sinful nature. With that come thoughts inserted by demons into our minds to tempt us to sin. When we give in, the dross settles in our hearts.

The cross must then be applied anew in our lives. Jesus saved us once and for all; yet He saves us continually, for we sin against His laws and His holiness many times. Whenever an offense has been committed, it must be cleansed. It can be cleansed by no act of penitence on our side and no amount of sacrifice or discipline. The heart is cleansed only by the blood of the Lamb.

Satan has been around since the beginning of creation. He has studied human behavior for thousands of years. He knows the power of a pure heart, and he is very intent on trying to keep us in the mire and somewhat "safe" and neutralized. Therefore, we should not be surprised at his tactics, but we do need to recognize his common inroads and give him no chance to hinder our fellowship with the Father.

To keep believers from applying the blood, the enemy heaps up guilt and shame against them. Satan is the accuser, and he loves to point out just how much we have sinned, how unworthy we are to serve a holy God, and how He must have had enough of us. He points out our failures in service and our weaknesses, and he makes us feel generally miserable about ourselves and our performance.

This is an ugly trick, because it insinuates that we are accepted or rejected based on our service. The accusation is directed toward *our* worthiness, and it tries to make us accept our need for betterment by harder work, greater discipline, and greater humility. This is in complete contradiction to the message of the Gospel, and it never alleviates, but rather highlights, our perpetual shortcomings. This thinking opens the door for a religious spirit to enter and work death in us. The religious spirit feeds on the works of people to become acceptable to God and ignores the atonement of Christ. This road is utterly rejected by God and will never make us holy.

The way to diffuse the charges of satan is not to defend ourselves, but to agree with him when he is right! Jesus said,

> *Settle matters quickly with your adversary who is taking you to court. Do it while you are still with him on the way, or he may hand you over to the judge, and the judge may hand you over to the officer, and you may be thrown into prison. I tell you the truth, you will not get out until you have paid the last penny* (Matthew 5:25-26).

Our adversary, in this case, is satan, and he is taking us to court by accusing us of wrongdoing. Jesus says that we must settle the charge brought against us. It is not enough to ignore it and forget; it must be dealt with quickly, or it will come back to hurt us later.

We know ourselves that we sin, that we fail, that our works are imperfect and our service incomplete. We know that we many times take the road of selfishness instead of walking in love toward others. The accusations bring condemnation because there is some truth to them.

So we agree with the accuser and confess our guilt before God, acknowledging that what he says is right. But then we set our eyes on the Son of God, who has already born our punishment and is releasing us from all charges. Because we put our hope in *His* righteousness and not our own, we receive *His* purity in the place of our guilt. We are clean, and by the ruling of the court of Heaven, we are acquitted. The accusations against us have been legally settled; the case is closed.

As we can see from this hearing, we must approach His throne to confess our sins to receive the provided pardon. *If we confess our sins He is faithful and just and will forgive us our sins and purify us from all unrighteousness* (1 John 1:9).

It is when we confess that we meet the mercy of God and are cleansed and made right with Him. If we hide our sins, we are not really acknowledging them as sins needing His forgiveness. Then they become a backdoor into our lives through which demons can plague our conscience with guilt.

The same goes with our sins toward one another. A clean heart is a heart that has no reason to hide. A husband or wife who starts withdrawing and having secrets from the spouse is one who will be open to torment and alienation. A believer who withdraws from a brother or sister because of an offense is vulnerable to attacks from the enemy. It is necessary to keep short accounts so that satan will be given no room to cause division and alienation in the Church. Just as we are forgiven by God for the sake of Jesus, so must we learn to forgive ourselves and forgive each other.

The enemy is a master of extremes. Some people sin big, and because their sin is so great, they settle in their hearts that they have gone too far and God cannot forgive them. Others sin in very small ways, and because their offense is so small they judge it too small to be brought up and dealt with. Some people have been abused and hurt to such degrees that they feel they are not able to forgive. Others brush away the hurt they feel over some minor offense and will not acknowledge the stab they feel. But just as God is able to deal with the elephants, so must He be allowed to deal with *the little foxes that ruin the vineyards"* (Song of Sol. 2:15). The pure heart seeks forgiveness and honestly forgives, whether large or small, and finds the beauty of healing on the other side.

To possess a clean heart takes a measure of honesty on our sides, honesty about ourselves and about others. The honest heart agrees that sin is sin and must be dealt with, but it also accepts the grace and mercy that God offers to help it overcome. The pure heart does not clean its house by brushing things under the carpet to be forgotten. Instead, it uncovers all the dirt and filth of the past and present and determines to have it all gone, all covered by the blood, the only sin-cleaner that does the job.

Have you done your big spring cleaning yet?

PERSONAL REFLECTION

1. What are some bad traits on my mother's side of the family that seem to be generational?

2. What are some traits on my father's side of the family that are destructive?

3. What are some things in my behavior or physical weakness that I know come from a family line?

4. Where could I get information on my family history, in particular explaining to me where these traits could have their roots?

5. If I could choose one thing in my family to be changed by God, which one would it be, and what are the things I think would be affected by this change?

6. In the next six months, what could I do to get more experience and understanding of my own and other cultures (especially the spiritual authority that rules it)?

7. What are some things in my own culture that I already detect as an evil infiltration to keep my nation from knowing God?

8. My strategy for training my mind is:

9. Do I still carry wounds of the past that need to be cleansed? Do I still feel some major hurdles in forgiving myself and others?

10. What could be some of the minor offenses that I have allowed to slip by without dealing with them properly?

ENDNOTES

1. A prayer of confession and repentance can break generational sins and bondages. As we are made aware of the sin of a parent or grandparent, we pray against this sin and stop its influence over our lives. For example, *"Lord, I confess the sins of my grandmother, who was involved in witchcraft and worked against your Holy Spirit. I renounce all wickedness that has been passed from her to me, and I break, in the authority of my Lord, any curse it placed on my life. Spirit of witchcraft, I deny you entry and any hold on my life. I claim the power of the blood of Jesus to save and cleanse me. In the name of Jesus, my Savior, amen."* The wording is not the important thing; what is important is that we speak and name that which we repent of and state in whose authority we stand. It is likely that we are standing against a spirit

that has been attached to our family for years and that is not willing to let go. Although it may still have power over other family members, we have protection and authority as believers to resist its influence over us.

2. George Otis Jr. shares in his book *Informed Intercession* many such stories of transformation. He is the founder of The Sentinel Group, a research group that chronicles divine transformation of land and peoples. Visit their Website at www.TransformNations.com.

CHAPTER TEN

DISCIPLINES OF A SOLDIER

If anyone would come after Me, he must deny himself and take up his cross daily and follow Me. For whoever wants to save his life will lose it, but whoever loses his life for Me will save it (Luke 9:23-24).

Your attitude should be the same as that of Christ Jesus: who, being in very nature God, did not consider equality with God something to be grasped, but made Himself nothing, taking the very nature of a servant, being made in human likeness. And being found in appearance as a man, He humbled Himself and became obedient to death—even death on a cross (Philippians 2:5-8).

THE WAY OF THE CROSS

The cross that Jesus talks of is the crucifying of the flesh—our sinful nature. In the same way that Jesus died, carrying in His body the sins of humankind, so also we must learn to live a life of denying the flesh from having its way. And the only way that will happen is by putting it to death.

Left to ourselves, we would have no chance to see our flesh dead. We want too much; we need too much; we are completely self-centered in how we think and act. But because of the mercy of God, He provided us with a solution. He gave us a cross to bear and a Man to follow. The Holy Spirit works mightily in us to change our self-centeredness to Christ-centeredness, giving us His attitude. We must put this attitude on like a servant's apron, ready for daily tasks, and not take it off until the day is done. Day by day by day we get up to offer ourselves to the Lord. *I am Yours. I accept all that comes from Your hand; do with me what brings glory to Your name and fulfills Your perfect will. How shall I serve You today? What have You given me to care for? Let me become excellent in my service. You are worthy of my life.*

As I was pondering the heart attitude of the Lord facing *His* cross, the following thoughts ministered powerfully to me. The Lord was completely human on one level, yet so great in the strength of His resolve to complete His race—in all ways identifying with the weaknesses of a mortal body and the earthly life we all have to live through, thus showing us that with God we can all overcome.

God and satan push us to the cross—they both want us dead! Satan wants to destroy us; God wants us to bear the fruit of a yielded life.

Carrying our cross is counted as worship. Romans 12:1-2 says to offer our bodies as living sacrifices—and this in itself is worship! A life and attitude surrendered to God's rule and daily direction, that will not listen to the protests and pleas of the flesh, brings glory and great joy to the Father.

To die to ourselves is painful. Jesus did not enjoy His cross! His whole body rose up against the painful trial waiting for Him. His struggle with

His human nature—though unspoiled by sin—was in Gethsemane, and it was hard. His sweat turned to blood in the face of the coming separation from holiness and His Father's presence, yet He was determined to save the human race. When He surrendered to His Father's will, He was again at peace. The physical experience of the cross itself did not shake Him; He had already fought His battle.

The cross will never be easy. It is designed to kill your flesh, and the flesh will always protest. The only way to conquer is by resisting our flesh—our own desires, needs, and wants—and stubbornly holding fast to the goodness of the One who calls us while walking forward.

The cross is continuously inconvenient to pick up, and the decision to surrender has to be made moment by moment, day after day. When we carry our cross in the right attitude, we will display His composure: peace, serenity, willingness, and patience, and our eyes will be fixed on the goal beyond the cross. If this is not our attitude, then we may need to evaluate our situation. What are we actually carrying?

The cross is not the end. The goodness of God is revealed after we surrender and "die"; then God works the resurrection! Ephesians 1:19-21 says that God's divine power for us who believe is like the mighty power that He exercised when He raised Jesus from the dead. The yielded life is where God's power starts manifesting itself in us.

The cross must have its course. Just as the Lord, even upon surrendering His will, had to endure the whipping, the scorn, the road to Golgotha, the crucifixion, and the hours on the cross, so the cross must have its way with us. Some roads are longer, some shorter. The Lord determines how long we must endure and when His work has been completed. Jesus stayed alive and in pain on the cross until He knew His task was completed; then He breathed His last and died. Why was His time not shortened an hour? We do not know. But at the time of death Jesus declared, *"It is finished"* (John 19:30). The work of the cross had been completed. We must learn to trust the Father for our times.

The cross yields a great harvest. Finally, the cross is the ultimate display of the divine *principle of the seed.* Jesus said, while predicting His own death, *"Unless a kernel of wheat falls to the ground and dies, it remains only a single seed. But if it dies, it produces many seeds. The man who loves his life will lose it, while the man who hates his life in this world will keep it for eternal life"* (John 12:24-25). If we want to produce a crop, we must embrace the way of the cross and be willing to walk the way the Father chooses for us. Then we will also be raised to see the yield from our lives. Then this promise will be ours:

> *Those who sow in tears will reap with songs of joy. He who goes out weeping, carrying seeds to sow, will return with songs of joy, carrying sheaves with him* (Psalm 126:5-6).

THE THREE DISCIPLINES

In the Sermon on the Mount, found in Matthew 5–7, Jesus lays down some basic principles of conduct for His Kingdom. In this discourse we find three disciplines that Jesus' followers will practice. These three disciplines are *prayer, fasting,* and *giving.*

PRAYER

Prayer is very simply spending time with God. The more the truth sinks in that He sees us as His children, now that we are saved, the more we relax and learn to come as we are. We have nothing to prove. God knows all there is to know about us, and He still loves us. He is *Papa*—we respect and love Him at the same time, daring to come at any time and for any reason.

Prayer is one of the most powerful weapons we have to make war against the kingdom of darkness. We are small in the great scheme of things, and the enemy is strong. Our prayers appeal to the One who is stronger, the One who places our enemies under our feet and who delivers us from all evil.

The subject of prayer seems to bring up more feelings of guilt and inadequacy than almost any other topic among Christians. We all know that we are supposed to pray, and yet we pray so little. Even when we pray more, we still might feel that we have not prayed enough. This again is a tactic from the enemy to keep us focused on our own performance rather than enjoying our fellowship with the Father.

Through prayer, Father God has opened up a new world for us, the heavenly one. It is His Kingdom and His home, and He wants us to start feeling at home there with Him. Just as when we grow up in our parents' home, there are many things going on every day. Home is where we find out what our day will look like. Home is where we learn to work and be faithful. Home is where we eat and play and have fun. Home is where we are disciplined, loved, and forgiven. Prayer opens the door for us to step into Papa's presence and into our true home. *Not* praying is like going on a prolonged sleepover in the world, getting more and more accustomed to its ways and more and more estranged from our real identity and family.

The Lord accepts the way we come to Him; He made us unique. Prayer does not come in a format that all His children must follow. Some of us will be strong in the memorizing of Scripture and declaring His truth. Some spend much time crying out for people they love and are concerned for. Some are constantly constructing or making plans for the future and come to discuss details. Some are carefree and dance and sing. Some are burdened by many responsibilities and come to seek help and strength for their tasks. We come as we are to meet with Papa. He does not want us to come in any other way.

FASTING

The next discipline is *fasting*. Fasting is when we go without food for a season to spend time before the Lord. It is not used at just any time and for just any reason. It is *set apart for breakthrough*. We deny ourselves one necessary thing (food) to gain the answer, the strength or the healing we seek.

In Matthew 6:16 we find Jesus saying, *When* we fast. It is something His people will do from time to time. Matthew 9:15 clarifies that fasting does not coincide with joy and celebrations, but is used in times of mourning or desperation. When our situation is such that it requires an answer from God, then we fast.

When a woman is getting ready to deliver a baby, food is most of the time not an option. The last hours are dedicated to breathing and birthing. Even talking becomes difficult. Every ounce of strength is directed to helping the baby move down the birth canal and have a safe arrival. But after the birth there is an instant relief from the pain, and there is joy and celebration and phone calls with the good news. And for the mother, there is food and rest!

Fasting is to take part in a birthing process. It is painful and uncomfortable, and many times we cannot wait until it is over. Yet we go through it. So did the Lord. The cross was a long, painful fast to birth His Bride. There are seasons when we desperately need His touch, His breakthrough, His directions, and His comfort. We fast to free ourselves from old sluggish mindsets and that which holds us back in order to reach for the hand of God—*"If I only touch His cloak, I will be healed!"* (See Matthew 9:20.)

Second Chronicles 16:9 says, *"For the eyes of the Lord range throughout the earth to strengthen those whose hearts are fully committed to Him."* A fast declares to the invisible realm *Who* we anchor our hope on. Therefore, as we submit our well-being into the hands of the Lord, ceasing to make provisions for our own needs, we place ourselves squarely in the path of a move of God. He is Jehovah Jireh, *the God who provides.*

How do we fast? One fast can look very different from another, and usually the severity of the fast matches the desperation of our hearts; when we are in need of a greater miracle, we do a greater fast. Still, a fast is a voluntary act on our side, and we decide what we will give up.

When we decide to fast, we first decide on its objective and with it an assigned scope and time frame. Being clear about our commitment helps us stick to our course when our bodies start protesting.

A fast means that we abstain from food. A full fast means to not eat or drink anything but water, and a partial fast means to abstain from a certain kind of food or foods. In between these fasts is a broad place of freedom and personal choice of what and how much we feel the need to give up. As we said earlier, desperation dictates our decisions. I have put together a reference list for the new "faster," to give ideas of what a fast can look like in different scenarios. The goal for a beginner is to get a taste for the goodness of God in meeting us when we seek Him earnestly and not to get burned on stringent commitments. We are free to learn, make mistakes, and grow in understanding and use of this asset among our weapons against darkness!

Fasting:

- *One specific meal per week*—For a long-term desire (such as revival, a change in the law, ongoing perseverance and vision in our tasks, an unsaved family member, and so forth).

- *Twenty-four hours*—For breakthrough of an imminent need or crisis (such as a very sick family member, an upcoming meeting where we will minister, financial breakthrough, and so forth).

- *Life fast*—Giving up one or more food items (meat, soda, coffee, ice cream) until there is a change (such as the end of abortion in the country, a family member saved, the release of a spiritual gift we are asking for, and so forth).

- *Three days*—Specific prayer target or need of greater proportion (healing, victory over a spiritual bondage or generational sin, or direction or confirmation for moves, education, or calling).

- *Longer fasts, up to 40 days*—Banding together with other believers and sharing a common burden for the city, nation, or a specific subject (such as abortion, revival, and so forth). Depending on what we are able to contribute, we may fast one meal a day, two meals a day, or fast continually, but still drink liquids or soups.

If we need to break a fast before the time, it is good to have an accountability partner to talk with. There is a lot of freedom in fasting, but it *is* a discipline, and it is a commitment before the Lord. After we learn through experience what to expect from our bodies, our minds, our families, and the Lord, we will find that fasting helps us grow stronger and more focused in our calling. Though fasting is a sacrifice, it comes with definite and long-lasting rewards.

GIVING

The third discipline is *giving.* Again Jesus says, *"When..."* we give—we are called to be generous and give freely, just as the Father has poured out His goodness on us. He promises to bless us as we learn to give (see Matt. 6:2).

> *Give, and it will be given to you. A good measure, pressed down, shaken together and running over, will be poured into your lap. For with the measure you use, it will be measured to you* (Luke 6:38).

It is not people who are asking us to give—it is God. The God who created the earth with all its resources and who needs nothing is the One who asks us to give (see Mal. 3:10). Since He obviously does not need us to give for His sake, He must be asking us to give for other reasons. I think giving is mostly for *our* benefit, although it blesses others and fills up God's storehouse (the Church) for the works of God. Let us look at some aspects of what giving does to us, the giver.

Giving frees us from fear. Giving is a statement of trusting God to provide, and it denies our fallen nature the urge to trust in the god of gold. Although there is nothing wrong with being successful in business and finances, to *hoard* wealth is a sign of insecurity and self-preservation. It indicates a lack of faith in and understanding of the God who pays attention to even the smallest of His creatures and has promised to clothe and feed us—every day (see Matt. 6:31-33). We have no reason to fear.

Giving blesses us. The Lord says in His Word that we can test Him on this—He is good to hold to His end of the bargain. If we are faithful to give back to Him what He asks for—10 percent of our income, called a *tithe*—He promises to open up the skies of provision for us (see Mal. 3:10-12). For those who struggle with life insurance and health insurance plans—this is *God's* simple plan: *give, and it will be given to you.* Having grown up in a large family with one small income, I can testify that God blessed us because my parents tithed. We stayed strong and healthy, and we never lacked food. The household machines and the cars seldom caused trouble. When we had need of something big—like a better vehicle—the Lord had His way of sending it our way free of charge.

Giving challenges us. We cannot out-give God—impossible! On many levels He will bless us financially and materially when we tithe, but truly His blessings for us go far beyond those temporary provisions. If we set our eyes on the Lord and stop worrying about our needs and how they will be met and instead focus on serving His desire—then our needs fall into their rightful place behind our backs (out of our sight). Although a man is set to provide for his family, he is commanded not to worry (see Matt. 6:31). We are all meant to serve the Lord, not our wants. All work has its place—but we must seek the Lord first. He makes all other things fall into place.

These three disciplines—prayer, fasting, and giving—are simple and profound ways we impact those around us and the world. We ourselves are changed in the process! Jesus has handed us the secrets of the Kingdom of Heaven (see Matt. 5-7; 13:11). Oh, may they be our greatest treasure in this life!

THE BOUNDARIES OF OUR CALLING

Lord, You have assigned me my portion and my cup; You have made my lot secure. The boundary lines have fallen for me in pleasant places; surely I have a delightful inheritance (Psalm 16:5-6).

Putting our lives in the Lord's service is exciting. We have an imaginative, omnipotent Master who knows all about us and who knows where to place us to give us joy and utilize our talents. But putting ourselves under His command also means restrictions. We cannot live for ourselves anymore; someone else is in charge, and whether glorious or torturous, we are committed to following our Leader's orders.

From Psalm 16, we read that David found that God had set boundaries around him. Because he trusted in God's goodness, he was not dismayed at his limitations, but rejoiced instead. We can rebel against boundaries and feel hemmed in and stifled; at other times we recognize that boundaries were placed by Someone who loved us enough to protect us, just as we protect our children with rules. Our task is to learn where God has set our personal boundaries and remain in them.

Our first boundary is our physical body and limited time and resources. When we do not heed these boundaries, we head for burn-out. When we are young, we are often eager to charge any obstacle to use or prove our strength. The older we get, the more we recognize our physical limitations (that keep growing!) and become more careful in choosing what to spend our resources on.

Our second boundary is God's Word. The more we read and meditate on His Word, the more we know what boundaries God has placed around us. The Old Testament was written largely for the reason of clarifying God's boundaries around humankind. To sin is to step over one of the boundary lines God has set up. We may not know that we are stepping over a spiritual line by sinning, but we step over, nonetheless. Whether we do it ignorantly or willfully, we are liable to be punished. All the commands that Christ gave the Church are boundaries. When we follow them, we are safe and stay under His protection. When we step over the line, we also step out from under His covering in that area and are open targets for the enemy (see Deut. 28).

Our third boundary is our calling. There are a million good things we *could* do with our lives, but we are not meant to do them. We are not responsible for the world, nor to meet all its needs. We are called to follow Jesus. He stated His calling in this way, *"My food is to do the will of Him who sent Me and to finish His work"* (John 4:34).

Jesus lived within the boundaries of His Father's will. He did not heal all the time, although there were plenty of demands on His time. He did not take off on mass crusades, although He certainly had the words to rock the world! What did He do? He listened to His Father and did what the Father requested of Him. God showed Jesus the path He was to walk, and He submitted to it.

Jesus said that He sends us in the same way the Father sent Him (see John 20:21). He has a master plan, a blueprint for our lives. As we lay ourselves on the altar of service, He reveals the path He has for us. Good-bye, independence. Welcome, life of the cross, the life submitted to the will of the Lord.

It can be a scary thing to lie down on an altar apart from our own choice. But He is our Beloved, the One who saved us by laying down His own life. He has our best in mind. The road He chooses for us will certainly involve pain, but the end result will be glory. Have you ever prayed: *I am Yours, Lord, change me at whatever cost, and make me like your Son Jesus?* He heard that prayer, and this is the answer: *Get on the altar, My son, My daughter. Let Me take away from you, little by little, all that is not from Me, and let Me prune those areas in you that are not bearing much fruit. Accept My boundaries and receive My protection; accept My will and follow it. I am faithful; I will see to it that the end of this road is life and joy for you.*

On the altar we lose our lives for His sake, but we find that He gives them back to us with amazing results. He places us in the plan that He has had for us from the beginning, the one for which He custom-made us. After we tearfully say goodbye to our own dreams and desires, He starts rearranging our lives and putting them in order, the dreams and desires in the place for which He first planted them in our hearts. *"Delight yourself in the Lord, and He will give you the desires of your heart"* (Ps. 37:4). We find that after we stop running after our own desires and start pursuing His call, He hands them back to us with His blessing! *Whoever finds his life will lose it, and whoever loses his life for My sake will find it* (Matt. 10:39).

WONDERFUL FORGIVENESS

To forgive may well be one of the hardest things we will ever learn to do. It is costly and precious and painful, but it will reap a harvest of peace for us.

When someone has offended us, hurt us, or sinned against us, the pain is real and needs attention. We have three options:

1. *We can leave it unattended.* Unattended wounds will either be in a climate of healing (we love enough to disregard the offense and forget the incident), or they become infected and more severe than they were from the beginning.

2. *We recognize our hurt, but forgive the offender.* We relinquish our right for vengeance and refuse to play God (the rightful Judge) in the situation. We decide to not hold anything against the offender and release him or her from their debt toward us. We acknowledge that they are guilty, that they owe us an apology and restitution, but we forgive them their debt.

3. *We can hold on to our hurt and not offer forgiveness.* This is not cruelty on our side; it is justice—they sinned, and they should pay for it. We want to see them punished, because they hurt us; we want them to "get what they deserve." We want revenge or restitution, either by inflicting it ourselves or seeing the matter dealt with some other way.

Let me use an illustration to show what happens spiritually when we do not forgive our offenders.

Spiderman can shoot spider webs, sticky strings that grab hold of a surface and allow him to flip his full body weight around. He attaches himself to a surface until he decides to release his hold. Now, imagine your offender as a bad Spiderman, but instead of *him* having a release mechanism for his strings, God has handed it to *you*.

When someone sins against us, they attach themselves through their actions to our souls. As long as we do not forgive them, we stay attached. The offenders can beg our forgiveness, but they cannot disentangle themselves from us—we are the ones who decide over the release button. When we forgive, we "loose" the offenders from our judgments and our right to revenge, and we free both ourselves and the offenders from the grip of the invisible attachment that kept us bound. We may think we are doing the other people a great favor by letting them go, but truly we are helping ourselves even more. When we do not forgive, we bind ourselves to our pain and anger, and our souls are not free.

Jesus said, "...*What you bind on earth will be bound in heaven, and what you lose on earth will be loosed in heaven*" (Matt. 16:19). He also said that we must forgive each other or God Himself will not forgive us; we become bound by our own device (see Matt. 6:14-15). The reason for the Lord's tough stance in this matter is laid out in *the Parable of the Unmerciful Servant* (see Matt. 18:21-35). In this parable a king is settling accounts with his servants. One of them owes him millions of dollars, but cannot pay. Because the man begs for mercy, the king has compassion on him and cancels his debt. The freed servant then turns around and demands that another man repay for some miniscule debt by comparison—about a hundred days' wages. Instead of showing him mercy, the man sees that he gets thrown in prison until the debt is paid off. When the king hears of this, he is very angry and throws the unmerciful servant into prison as well, where he will stay until his full debt is paid off. Jesus concludes the parable by saying, "*This is how My heavenly Father will treat each of you unless you forgive your brother from the heart*" (Matt. 18:35).

Since God is so abundantly merciful toward us, it pains Him to see us so stingy and legalistic in our approach to others. Why do we hold on to petty offenses and bind ourselves to them when He forgave us all our sins and with that gives us all He has? Mercy should give birth to mercy.

As a follower of Jesus, the Lord gives you the power to release your offender before the Heavenly Judge.

> *Again Jesus said, "Peace be with you! As the Father has sent Me, I am sending you." And with that He breathed on them and said, "Receive the Holy Spirit. If you forgive anyone his sins, they are forgiven; if you do not forgive them, they are not forgiven"* (John 20:21-23).

This is a great responsibility. Jesus gives us the authority to change our offender's records on the Judgment Day! If someone cheats us, for example, Jesus asks us what we want done. If we forgive the deed, the Lord cancels the charge; it will not be mentioned again. If we do not forgive, the charge will be brought up and receive its punishment. Of course, we bind ourselves to our offender's fate—the way we judge or show mercy becomes the Lord's measuring rod when He deals with us, as well (see Matt. 7:1-2).

Evildoers and unbelievers will not escape just punishment because of our mercy. We only released them from the part of the charge that was ours to forgive. But our willingness to show forgiveness could save our adversary, if he would heed the kindness and turn to the Lord. If he does not, he will face the outcome of his own decisions (see Isa. 26:10-11). At the closing of the matter, we find that the mercy we showed stored up mercy for us on that Day.

THE LONELY ROAD

> *Blessed is the man who perseveres under trial, because when he has stood the test, he will receive the crown of life that God has promised to those who love Him* (James 1:12).

There is a path in God's training program for His soldiers that will never be pleasant or willingly chosen. Yet it is necessary, and it has the potential of bearing the sweetest fruit. I call it *the lonely road.* It is the road of righteous suffering.

Proverbs 14:10 says, *"Each heart knows its own bitterness; and no one else can share its joy."* There comes a time when the Lord leads us into trials and hardships, and however many friends we have, we still have to go through it alone, leaning only on the Lord. The condition of loneliness in itself is the first trial that brings about change in us. It dramatically increases our felt need for the Lord, His presence, and His words of counsel and wisdom.

Pain causes us to look over our foundation. It is common to run in all directions and be busy at all times. Trials and pain bring us to a halt, and we start processing life again. We come to a place where we start listening to the Lord's voice instead of running to friends for sympathy or being too busy to hear or learn what He wants to teach us.

There are three main paths on this road of suffering.

The first path is physical weakness or sickness. Although the Lord's heart is always for our healing, we live in a fallen world. Our physical bodies manifest this through aging, ailing, and losing strength and ability. Sin is another cause for sickness; being out of alignment with God's will and out of bounds with His order invites sickness into our bodies. We can also become sick because of direct attacks from the enemy. All these things were not a part of the original design, and the Lord is grieved as He sees us struggle to be whole. His desire is that we will become whole in every way—body, soul, and spirit—and He has made provision for this through Jesus. We can be miraculously healed, restored, and delivered in an instant by the touch of His hand.

When the Lord tarries to heal us, we are faced with the choice to succumb to the trap of the enemy and doubt the character and goodness of God or to submit ourselves to our Creator and accept the challenge of faith. Do we believe that He not only can heal, but that He cares enough to heal us? Yes! Are we willing to surrender ourselves not only to His goodness, but also to His ultimate plan—even if that means continued suffering and illness? Therein lies our righteous suffering—we must learn to trust God enough to allow Him to do His work in His time and to work with Him to see it completed in us. Our attention shifts from the desire to be free from pain to glorifying God in our bodies. His answer will come. In the meantime, what will we do?

The place of pain is lonely, but as we hold our Father's hand we find comfort in the truth that He will not let the trial be wasted. As we keep our eyes fixed on Him, to love Him and offer our lives up before Him, we find grace to persevere.

> *Therefore, since Christ suffered in His body, arm yourselves also with the same attitude, because he who has suffered in his body is done with sin* (1 Peter 4:1).

The second path on the road of suffering is persecution. Persecution is to be on satan's blacklist, the ones he is hunting down to destroy. In many parts of the world persecution is physical, with beatings and torture and horrendous living conditions.

Chinese Christians are some of the most persecuted people in the history of the Church. They also have an incredible testimony of perseverance and of miraculous escapes and divine encounters.[1] Church history testifies to the amazing result of persecution; the death of God's people has not caused the Church to lose ground, but rather to thrive, adding fervor to her determination to preach the Gospel. Persecution tests and refines our faith and brings glory to God.

> *…Now for a little while you may have had to suffer grief in all kinds of trials. These have come so that your faith—of greater worth than gold, which perishes even though refined by fire— may be proved genuine and may result in praise, glory and honor when Jesus Christ is revealed* (1 Peter 1:6-7).

In the West, persecution is not as blatant, but it is still there. Whether we have to stand our ground in our schools or colleges against an intimidating crowd or are sued for preaching the Word of God in our churches, perse-cution will be a daily occurrence in the world as long as the enemy is on the loose. Jesus said we should expect this to happen; we will be hated by the same enemy that hated and persecuted Him (see John 15:18-20). In the midst of this, He will pour out His Spirit on us in such measure that it will astound onlookers and encourage the saints. Words will be given us to speak, boldness will come on us and remove all timidity, and joy will over-flow in the midst of suffering (see Mark 13:11; Acts 4:21,31; 5:41).

The third path is the suffering that comes from carrying our cross; it is the accumulation of every surrender and choice we make throughout our days, months, years, and lifetime of doing the Lord's will and not our own. Many times others cannot see the difference of doing a job and doing it in surren-der to His call; but *we* know, and *He* sees.

The twofold command of the cross is to deny ourselves and to carry what God gives us to carry (see Luke 9:23). *No one else is called to carry my cross but me* (see Gal. 6:5). Sometimes we make the mistake of thinking that someone near us is meant to help us carry our cross, but it is not so. We are blessed to have someone nearby who stoops to bear some of our burden, but this is a grace on their side.

The cross is a call to *separation.* It is not easy for a human being to live in the world and yet learn to not spiritually drink its waters. Neither is it easy to cut away our old ties and habits when the Lord asks us to move to higher ground. This separation from what we were used to can produce a deep sense of loneliness.

The road of righteous suffering can be confusing at times. Satan will do his best to condemn us, like Job's friends trying to persuade him of being guilty. While satan uses our cross to accuse us, God uses it to prove our worth. *But He knows the way that I take; when He has tested me, I will come forth as gold* (Job 23:10).

These are some things that emerge in the midst of our trials.

THE FRUIT OF RIGHTEOUS SUFFERING

- Sin will lose its luster and desire over us.

- The fear of man will diminish and fade away.

- The fear of God will increase.

- Our thirst for God and His ways will cause rapid growth.

- The fruit of the Spirit in us will become sweeter and more evident.

- Our weakness will magnify His overshadowing grace and power.

- Our desire for the momentary and physical will wane.

- It will yield to the desire for the invisible and eternal.

- Our friendship and walk with the Lord will be deeper.

- Dependence on the Holy Spirit will increase.

- Dependence on people and our own resources will decrease.

- We will appreciate other's help and kindness much more.

- And thankfulness for the Lord's kindness and mercy will abound.

HEART OF A WARRIOR

There is an attitude that makes us overcome obstacles and become champions for God's Kingdom. That is the attitude that says, *"I have counted the cost. Whatever comes, it is worth it—my King is worth it."* It is the heartbeat of a warrior who delights in challenges and excels under pressure, knowing that he is running for a great reward. The realization of enemies surrounding him and plans devised against him does not cause him to cower, but to straighten and fight with even greater resolve. He will not give up, back off, or turn around; he has chosen to serve His King until death.

This kind of attitude and heart is not developed over night, but if we desire to develop a warrior's heart, we are setting our eyes on a noble goal. In a world of increasing darkness, where principalities and demonic strongholds are constantly being built and fortified, God is calling those who will listen to learn the road of the warrior. King David had his mighty men, great men of valor, any one of whom could slay hundreds of enemies and break through enemy defenses. We have Jesus, the son of David, the King of kings, and with Him the eternal Kingdom to live and die for. Will you give Him your heart, your commitment, and your sword? Whether young or old, man or woman, rich or poor, learned or unschooled—He can train you and make you a *mighty man*, a spiritual warrior. We are not brave or strong enough to call ourselves to this task. Rather, ask yourself: *Is this what He wants for me?* Then walk forward in the confidence that *He who called you is faithful, and He will do it* (see 1 Thess. 5:24).

The Lord has blessed me with a husband who developed the heart of a warrior. I would like to share the story of his development with you. It is the story of God taking a broken young man and calling him to lay hold of Heaven. What God did for him, He is more than able to do for any of us as we apply ourselves to our training.

When Jeff was 5 years old, his parents divorced. From then on, he lived with his mother in the city and spent time on the farm with his father on weekends and in the summers. Although he went to church with his mother, it was just tradition to him.

The insecurity and the turmoil of his growing-up years, coupled with his spiritual void, made him prime target for becoming involved in sin to fill his needs. But at the age of 19 he was radically saved through the visits of a door-to-door evangelist on his college campus, and the Lord started the process of healing his wounds.

The previous allurements gave way for what satisfied. He went jogging, away from all distractions, and learned to pour out his heart to this newly discovered heavenly Father. He felt so weak, so needy, and so messed up that he figured he had nothing to lose by giving himself completely over to trusting the Lord. In so doing, he quickly grew in his faith.

From these early years as a believer, the Lord started forming in Jeff the heart of a warrior. There were many combining factors that helped the formation, but what started the process was in separating himself from distractions to spend time with his Father, setting his heart to only pursue God. From this springboard of intimate fellowship and commitment he took several decisive steps.

He put himself in training. When he read the Scriptures, he noticed the discrepancies between what he was and what he should be, and he desired change. He saw the lazy attitude he had toward life, and he wrote the word *discipline* on a paper and hung it on the wall in his room, where he would be constantly reminded. He saw his ingrained selfishness and compared it to Philippians 2:3-4. He committed it to memory and made it his life verse. He knew he could not change himself and surrendered to the Lord. The Lord then began the work of changing him.

The next hurdle to overcome was the fear and insecurity he carried. He realized as he kept reading the Word, that these spirits would have no power over him unless he allowed them entry, so he began to refuse them power over him. He then recognized how satan had worked on him and his family in their unsaved condition, and he came to a point where he was angry enough to start fighting. He was drawn to literature and Bible verses that helped him understand and use his heavenly armor and his standing before God to break free from his past and start living by faith.

Next was a lesson in prayer vigilance. He started carrying around index cards to help remind him to pray for those he loved. Unsaved family members (which included most of them at that time) became a burden on his heart; he simply could not imagine Heaven without them. He determined to keep after the Lord in prayer until he saw breakthrough. It is a wonderful testimony in the family how many since then have come to the Lord.

After conversion Jeff wanted to know *how to make an impact for the Kingdom of God.* He became involved with FCA (Fellowship of Christian Athletes) on the campus. When some missionaries came around to speak in those meetings, he sought out more information. He committed himself to go wherever the Lord sent him and started going on mission trips. For every trip, the Lord sent him a little farther away and to harder places.

After graduating from college, he moved overseas on his first great venture—a two-year missions commitment to South Asia. There he was placed in circumstances that removed all familiar and comforting things from him. He was challenged with new languages, different and (in his opinion) not always so tasty food, some very different mind-sets of the people, painful illnesses, and his own personal weaknesses surfacing under the pressure. He had entered God's boot camp, tailor-made for Jeff Farwell.

The odds of making an impact were against him. The diet constantly upset his stomach. He had been placed as the only foreigner in a national team, where he faced daily challenges in communication and culture. The isolation from all familiar things pressed him even closer to Jesus and the reason for which he had decided to leave his home in the first place—to share the Good News to those who had not heard. He found that he could press through the intimidation of preaching and distributing Bibles on the streets in spite of Muslim opposition, and he pushed himself to keep going when there was no outward motivation—he *would* fulfill his goal!

After six months, he relocated to a nearby country. While trekking in the mountains to distribute Christian literature, he started meeting with resistance to what he was doing. He took this as sign that he was on to something worthy and kept going. Once his team was stopped by a border patrol and faced possible jail time. Though shaky on the inside, Jeff and his team member stood their ground; they would keep going despite the threats. Suddenly, they were released.

Later, as they trekked high on a mountain ridge, they realized that they were in for some severe monsoon rains. Jeff could feel the spiritual weight against them to stop their Gospel distribution. He knew the rains would potentially ruin their books and slow them down considerably. He could not accept this to be the Lord's will so he stood in faith and commanded the rain to stop. Although threatening overhead, the rain held off while the team hurried up the mountain side. As soon as they found safety and shelter, the downpour started.

The harder the circumstances and the greater the obstacles, the more obvious it became to Jeff that he needed to stand his ground and fight in whatever battle the Lord handed him. For every step of faith or stand he made, his confidence grew in the Lord's willingness to work in response to his prayers and lead him to victory. The more he had to confront the enemy, the more he came to understand his authority and responsibility to take up his sword and fight.

For us it is encouraging to realize that this heart of a warrior that the Lord saw fit to form in Jeff was not a matter of personality, but of training in character coupled with a stubborn determination to overcome.

Years later, Jeff found a group of similar-minded men who banded together to train in warfare together. This group of men adopted four important principles from Robert Lewis's book *Raising a Modern-Day Knight,*[2] which well describe both authentic manhood and the heart of a warrior. Lewis's four principles apply to men and women who are warriors in God's ranks:

1. *Reject passivity.* A warrior will not stand by and watch evil have its way. He will fight for the truth, for the helpless, and for the advance of the Kingdom.

2. *Accept responsibility.* A warrior accepts the mission and the calling of God and diligently applies himself to the training and the executing of his tasks.

3. *Lead courageously.* A warrior accepts that he is an example to those around him and will lead by his example of faith and courage.

4. *Expect a greater reward.* A warrior knows that his reward is with the King and will be revealed in time. He does not expect to be rewarded by men or in this life, but lives for eternal rewards.

We are not all going to face the same kind of battles. The Lord's boot camp looks different for each of us, forged by circumstances, family line, and calling. But the will of the King is that we all press forward and lay hold of our freedom and dispel the darkness we encounter. We may never be a national name or a known face here on earth. The important thing is that the Lord knows us. After our time of training, He will have another warrior to count on, one He can send to do His work and carry His light.

PERSONAL REFLECTION

1. What could I do to spur myself to obey the Lord more quickly and with a willing heart?

2. Do I present myself daily to serve God's purposes, or do I mostly do what I want to do during my day? Am I a faithful steward with the things (and people) God has given me to care for?

3. When I pray, do I feel burdened by self-imposed responsibilities, or do I enter prayer as a beloved child who wants to talk with my heavenly Father?

4. What are some *boundaries* God has placed around me? Are there any boundaries that I tend to break?

5. Is there anyone in my life (past or present) who I need to forgive? Is there anyone who I have sinned against or hurt? What should I do to bring healing to them?

6. What could I do to develop a warrior's heart? What could I do immediately to help me remember my resolve to become a warrior for God?

ENDNOTES

1. Read about Brother Yun in *The Heavenly Man*, by Brother Yun and Paul Hattaway (Oxford, England: Monarch Books, 2002); it is an incredible testimony to the power of God.

2. Robert Lewis, *Raising a Modern-Day Knight* (Carol Stream, IL: Tyndale House Publishers, 1997), 51–60.

A PERSPECTIVE ON THE PRESENT TIME

The training is done. I simply want to give my thoughts on the present time, as it is unfolding rapidly.

When Jesus faced the cross, He looked beyond the present suffering to its reward. He not only persevered with the heart of an overcomer, but also He saw the glory that would result from His endurance.

We have now come to a time when we are facing great evil being released on the Earth. In the midst of increasing darkness, the Lord is preparing us to meet Him as His Bride, spotless and pure. We are not placed in this time to grit our teeth and hope to not be detected by the enemy. We are called to cast aside all fear and prepare ourselves to meet our Lord.

When I was expecting my first child, I did not know what to expect from the labor and delivery. But ignorantly, I assumed that I would be a wonderful example of beautiful peace and be a tremendous witness to the nurses for the Lord. When labor set in for real, I was exhausted and unprepared for the level of pain that shot up. Instead of peace, I panicked! It was my unpreparedness that caused the biggest problem, since my expectation proved wrong.

The next pregnancy, I remembered the pain. I exercised with great focus, and kept my eyes firmly on conquering both my fear and the next delivery. When the day came, my will was set. As labor progressed, I kept reminding myself that it would get worse. When my little baby girl was born, I was actually surprised! I had expected more pain! This dear girl was named Joy, and in truth that day was a day of great joy.

How we will walk through the endtimes is much determined by our own expectations and mindset. The Lord does not forewarn us of a dark time so that we can ignore His warnings and hope to escape by hiding our heads in the sand. We need to heed the warnings and prepare ourselves for times of persecution and difficulty. Maybe the Lord will spare us; maybe we will not even feel the judgments that are coming on the world. It may be so; but while we hope for His kindness, we prepare for the trials that are just as precious as miraculous escapes. We must say in our hearts, *Whether I live or die, I am for the Lord.* This mindset will free us from fear and keep us active in doing what is good and right.

In all times of great trouble, God's people have placed their hopes in Heaven. When the African people were sold into slavery, they started creating Gospel songs of their heavenly hope, of which some are sung to this day. The beauty of their hope was magnified through their suffering. Years of slavery created a stubborn patience that would sing out in the dark, "You may put my body in chains, but my spirit is free and is soaring to my true home."

This kind of faith is so precious that it moves the Father's heart. The Lord Jesus said this in a vision to Rick Joyner:

> When My Father moves His little finger, the whole universe trembles. To shake the nations with your words does not impress anyone who dwells here. But when even the least

of My brethren on earth shows love, it brings joy to My Father's heart. When even the most humble church sings to My Father with true love in their hearts, He silences all of heaven to listen to them. He knows that one cannot help but to worship when they are beholding His glory here, but when those who are living in such darkness and difficulty sing with true hearts to Him, it touches Him more than all of the myriads of heaven can.

Many times the broken notes from earth caused all of heaven to weep with joy as they beheld My Father being touched. A few holy ones struggling to express their adoration for Him have many times caused Him to weep. Every time I see My brethren touch Him with true worship, it makes the pain and grief I knew on the cross seem like a small price to pay. Nothing brings Me more joy than when you worship My Father. It is in this worship that you, the Father, and I are all one.[1]

The believers of the early Church, as we can see in the epistles, set their hearts on the coming of the Lord and more than endured persecution; they thrived in the midst of it. The Chinese church in our time has been set as an example of enduring hardship. The constant threat on their lives has not dimmed their zeal, but has brought forth a great resolution to endure and spread the good news to the ends of the earth. In fact, when these persecuted brothers or sisters come to the West, they decline prayers for Chinese freedom. They see that the power and the help of God, together with the preaching of the Gospel, has been theirs because of their suffering.

In fact, many of these brave Chinese believers pity *us!* The lack of hardship has created in the Western church a jellylike fat around its heart that is very unhealthy. If we are put under pressure, we are conditioned to collapse rather than endure.

The Scriptures state that all fat belongs to the Lord (see Lev. 3:16). When we feed ourselves on the fat of the land, apart from acknowledging

His provisions, our hearts quickly become forgetful and unconcerned for our own condition and future, while the former vigilance and endurance fades. In truth, we are to be pitied. The Lord will have mercy on us, but He must now do it in His own way. He will burn up the fat. Many will collapse, having no good root, but some will be saved and find their hope re-awakened and their hearts cleansed to work properly once again. In our case, persecution is something we should welcome as mercy from the Lord. If we judge ourselves and our works, the Lord's judgments will not touch us.

THE PROPHETIC VOICE

As we enter into this time of increasing darkness, the Lord has given the Church an increasing light of prophetic words so that we may have His encouragement and be able to have our eyes fixed on the glories that are to come. This prophetic word is meant to be a light to help us stand firm with the increasing spiritual pressure of the air around us. To not accept this voice is dangerous, but how will we know the true voice from the voices of false prophets?

The only way to know the truth is to know the voice of Truth, which is Jesus Himself (see John 14:6). We must learn to know His voice. This book has equipped you for that very thing. I pray and hope that now you are starting to recognize the personal ways that He communicates with you. The more you practice His presence, eat His Word, and obey His voice, the easier it will be for you to recognize His voice. The Lord described this as being a sheep hearing his Shepherd's voice.

I heard a story from a man who had once observed shepherds and sheep in the East. There were three shepherds and three herds of sheep at the same watering hole. The herds were mingling, but when it was time for a shepherd to lead, he simply called his sheep, and they immediately separated themselves from the rest of the sheep and followed him. If a foreigner would have tried to call them, they would not have listened. They were in tune to only one voice, their own shepherd's.

In the same way, the only way we will know a prophet from a false prophet will be to recognize our Shepherd's voice in the words spoken. Even satan masquerades as an angel of light. He is a master of disguise, and he knows Scripture really well. Many wolves in sheep's clothing will come and try to infiltrate the Church, and those who do not know their Shepherd will easily be deceived.

I have faced such situations personally. Not having the gift of discernment, I kept listening to my husband as he sensed many things going on that I could not tell were happening. In the midst of us evaluating the situation, the Lord sent dreams to us, warning us of danger. Because we had learned to heed His voice, we escaped the net. But I was stupefied at how easy it would have been to just trust people! I had no indicator that anything was wrong except for the voice of the Lord. In the end, things surfaced that proved again the Lord's voice to be true. But if we had not heeded His voice, it might have been too late to avoid trouble.

Such times are upon us. True prophets will arise, because the Lord wants us to know what He is doing. But because of this aid against him, satan will do all he can to discredit this ministry by sending false prophets. Our only safe way through this is *not* to stop listening to the prophetic voice, but to draw closer to the Lord and listen to what He tells us personally. From that place we will be able to recognize who speaks from the Lord and who speaks from other sources.

The Lord said that the test of the validity of one of His servants will be seen by the fruit they produce (see Matt. 7:15-20). This is not the same as their works, which many times have been confused. There are many who have received extraordinary gifts of power by the Holy Spirit, and some of them are still operating in them, although they live in sin. Power easily corrupts. Satan will also give power to his servants. False prophets will rise up that do perform miracles of various kinds. Again, the Lord says to look at the fruit, not the works. A bad tree cannot produce good fruit, neither does a good tree produce bad fruit. What is done by the power of the Spirit will come and produce love, joy, peace, patience, kindness, goodness, gentleness, faithfulness, and self-control (see Gal. 5:22-23). Satan cannot produce good fruit; neither can his messengers. They will produce discord, confusion, hatred, impatience, ill report, manipulation, and control. These false prophets will cause problems to rise in the Church, not peace and unity.

In the end, the endorsement or rejection of a spokesperson is from the Lord Himself. John Bunyan is widely quoted as saying, *"If my life is fruitless, it does not matter who praises me, and if my life is fruitful, it does not matter who criticizes me."* I think that is worth taking to heart.

GOODBYE

Do you recall how you felt as you listened to or read the testimony of those who were faithful to God's calling in past times? Were you inspired by King David, or the faith of Abraham, the stories of Amy Carmichael or Hudson Taylor, the teaching and faith of John Wesley or Billy Graham? Have you decided who you want to get acquainted with in Heaven, those to whom you want to say, "Your life inspired me greatly in my own pursuit of God"? The wonderful thing is that they will know *your* name, too! Listen to this description of a man caught up in a vision to the throne room of God.

> My eyes were so fixed on the glory of the Lord that I walked a long time before I noticed that I was passing multitudes of people who were standing in ranks...As I looked at them, I had to stop. They were dazzling, more regal than anything I had ever seen. Their countenances were captivating.

> Never has such peace and confidence graced human faces. Each one was beautiful beyond earthly comparison. As I turned toward those who were close to me, they bowed in a greeting as though they recognized me.

> "How is it that you know me?" I asked, surprised at my own boldness in asking them a question.

"You are one of the saints fighting in the last battle," a man close by responded. "Everyone here knows you, as well as all those who are now fighting on the earth. We are the saints who have served the Lord in the generations before you. We are the great cloud of witnesses who have been given the right to behold the last battle. We know all of you, and we see all that you do."[2]

Do not forget your destiny and the time you are in. Do not let the world put you to sleep, even for a day. The time is growing very short. Fix your eyes on Jesus. Keep your eyes on the goal so that you will stand as an overcomer before Him. You are well-loved and well-known in the heavenly realms. It is time for you to take your place in the ranks.

I cheer for you!

ENDNOTES

1. Rick Joyner, *The Call* (Fort Mill, SC: MorningStar Publications, 2006), 145–146.

2. Rick Joyner, *The Final Quest* (Fort Mill, SC: MorningStar Publications, 2007), 95–96.

About Hanna E. Farwell

Jeff and **Hanna Farwell** spent several years serving the Lord in South Asia. They are now settled in Omaha, Nebraska. Jeff is establishing a House of Prayer, and Hanna writes books and homeschools their ten children. They are available for some speaking engagements on topics such as God's family planning, worship & spiritual warfare, revival, and dreams.

Hanna can be contacted at hanna2you@cox.net

Resource Information

Have you dared to trust God for your family size?

Make the transition from a culturally bound, misguided view of family planning to a vibrant, positive 'Yes!' to the God who loves all generations—ours and our children's.

Get ready to discover the power of an abandoned life in the hands of a faithful, almighty God, and find new faith to welcome the future and whomever He would send—in perfect season, in perfect number.

IN THE RIGHT HANDS, THIS BOOK WILL CHANGE LIVES!

Most of the people who need this message will not be looking for this book. To change their lives, you need to put a copy of this book in their hands.

> *But others (seeds) fell into good ground, and brought forth fruit, some a hundred-fold, some sixty-fold, some thirty-fold* (Matthew 13:8).

Our ministry is constantly seeking methods to find the good ground, the people who need this anointed message to change their lives. Will you help us reach these people?

> *Remember this—a farmer who plants only a few seeds will get a small crop. But the one who plants generously will get a generous crop* (2 Corinthians 9:6).

EXTEND THIS MINISTRY BY SOWING
3 BOOKS, 5 BOOKS, 10 BOOKS, OR MORE TODAY,
AND BECOME A LIFE CHANGER!

Thank you,

Don Nori Sr., Publisher
Destiny Image
Since 1982

DESTINY IMAGE PUBLISHERS, INC.

*"Speaking to the Purposes of God for This Generation
and for the Generations to Come."*

VISIT OUR NEW SITE HOME AT
WWW.DESTINYIMAGE.COM

FREE SUBSCRIPTION TO DI NEWSLETTER

Receive free unpublished articles by top DI authors, exclusive

discounts, and free downloads from our best and newest books.

Visit www.destinyimage.com to subscribe.

Write to: Destiny Image
             P.O. Box 310
             Shippensburg, PA 17257-0310

Call: 1-800-722-6774

Email: orders@destinyimage.com

For a complete list of our titles or to place an order
online, visit www.destinyimage.com.

FIND US ON FACEBOOK OR FOLLOW US ON TWITTER.

www.facebook.com/destinyimage   **facebook**
www.twitter.com/destinyimage   **twitter**

Printed in Great Britain
by Amazon